MW00817974

What People Are Saying about
James Donaldson and
Standing Above the Crowd

"Having worked with pro athletes in the major U.S. sports for forty-plus years, I respect my friend James Donaldson for accomplishing what is a very tall order. To stay true to your values, excel in your sport for many years, found and run a thriving business for more than two decades, all the while putting God and others first—James makes it look as easy as his dunks from way above the rim. When this smiling giant unpacks his amazing mind, it pays to look up and listen."

— George Toles, former NBA announcer and retired media executive

"James is a gentleman with heart. He cares deeply about his community and his friends old and new; I count myself lucky to be one of the latter. James inspired and encouraged me during our 2009 campaigns for local office, and I believe his words, 'If it's to be, it's up to me' will inspire others to live their best and stand tall beside him."

— Sally Bagshaw, Seattle City Council

"I knew James Donaldson as an opposing center with the NBA's Seattle SuperSonics and Dallas Mavericks when I was with the Los Angeles Lakers. We knew it would always be a tough contest because of his focus and sheer determination, and we would have to bring our "A" game."

— Jamaal Wilkes, Former NBA All-Star,
President/CEO of Jamaal Wilkes Financial Advisors, LLC

"Every day, James works to help his community by mentoring and teaching people how to make positive progress in their lives. His commitment to success isn't for self-gain; it's driven by his desire to see others achieve their goals and dreams. *Standing Above the Crowd* is one more example of how James reaches out to share his knowledge and experience for the benefit of others."

— W. Gregory Guedel, Attorney at Law, Foster Pepper, PLLC, and
Snohomish City Council Member

"*Standing Above the Crowd* makes me feel 10 feet tall!"

— Marlee Huber, author of *Unstoppable Abundance*

"Thank you for coming to my school today! When I heard we were having an assembly I was sort of disappointed....They tend to be boring. But when you were done speaking, I was yet again disappointed; but not because of the speech you gave, but because I didn't want for you to be done. What you were saying out there was really inspirational. I really did take something away from this assembly....I'd really like to hear more of what you've got to say, which brings me to ask about your book. I'd really like to read it myself."

— Katie Artt, high school student in Washington State

"I followed James' professional basketball career, and brimmed with pride to see him excel with the Dallas Mavericks and the Seattle Supersonics. I had a chance to connect with James to talk about his political aspirations, and how I could support his latest endeavor. I had a chance to get to know James as a person, and not just as a former opponent on the basketball court. I found James to be an intelligent man, who was dedicated to education and possessed a commitment to personal health and wellness, for not just himself, but for others as well. James is a deep thinker, and his insight provides us with something we can all learn and grow from."

— Kenneth R. Lyles, General Manager
Fishermen's Terminal/Maritime Industrial Center

"James Donaldson writes with a world of experience in many different fields. Read, enjoy, and then apply all of his insights and wisdom."

— Pat Williams, Orlando Magic senior vice president,
author of *Bear Bryant on Leadership*

"I have known James Donaldson since he was a Seattle SuperSonic. Since we saw each other regularly, I was in a unique position to watch James grow. It is easy to see externally how he has grown and succeeded, but I witnessed internal transformation. The growth on the outside pales with his spiritual growth."

— Stan Newell, D.P.M., .A.C.F.A.S

"If I had a million dollars to wager, I never would have bet that the words James Donaldson and NBA All-Star would have ever been uttered in the same sentence. Because of James' tremendous focus and drive to be a success, he consistently pushes himself to maximize his potential, and his book *Standing Above the Crowd* shows us all how to do the same."

— Marcus Johnson, NBA All-Star and former teammate

"James Donaldson is the most prolific and the most powerful figure of a Center the Mavericks have ever had (before or since his tenure in Dallas). I have known James Donaldson for over twenty years, and I was his tae kwon do Instructor during some of the greatest years in Mavs history. I was honored that James listened to me as a teacher, but he taught me plenty. One of the greatest things he showed me was the importance of his steadfast loyalty to his friends. I know that I can count on James and that he and I will always be friends."

— Kenn Thorpe, 5th Degree Tae Kwon Do Black Belt Instructor, Dallas, TX

"I had the opportunity to play in the NBA for a few years where I encountered the imposing James Donaldson. It wasn't until we both finished our careers in Europe that I saw James, the person, who had truly earned the title of Ambassador of Basketball by definitely "Standing Above the Crowd."

— Jerrod Mustaf, former NBA Player,
President of Street Basketball Association

"On the first day I met James Donaldson, he shared his personal philosophy on the values of hard work, perseverance, and education. James exemplifies the tenet that the starting point of all achievement is desire, which must remain a constant, because weak desires bring weak results. James' must-read book shares his positive life philosophy and views on the value of education that will help you to 'Stand Above the Crowd.'"

— Randy J. Aliment, Partner, Williams Kastner Law Firm

"Donaldson's thoughts expressed in *Standing Above the Crowd* are ideas that are above the crowds but below the clouds. James turns his readers onto some very positive concepts, which they can use not only personally, but also when dealing with others. Being a licensed behavioral health professional, I will suggest *Standing Above the Crowd* as reading material to several of my clients, especially those who are struggling with self-image issues or those who are having a hard time developing some life goals. My hope is that after reading *Standing Above the Crowd*, these patients might be motivated to use their unused talents and stand above the crowd."

— Chuck Wright, Licensed Mental Health Counselor, Licensed Marriage and Family Therapist, Certified Traumatic Stress Specialist

"I have known James since 1984, and through the years I have always felt that he was an extraordinarily intelligent man who would aspire to politics. I would not be surprised if he, one day in the near future, ran for President and won.....!!! "Just don't forget me, James."

— Harvey Catchings, Former NBA Player and Teammate

"*Standing Above the Crowd* reminds all of us of the tremendous potential we all possess and how to tap into it."

— Marvin Kunikiyo, D.C., author of *Revolutionizing Your Health*

"'Jimmy' (as I've always called him) has always been one to "Stand Above the Crowd." I remember as if it were yesterday that he would arrive early at the

Seattle SuperSonic practices and go through his drills that I taught him until he perfected them. Not many young players are willing to put in the time and effort that Jimmy did. That's one of the reasons that he had a twenty-year professional basketball career! His Desire, Dedication, and Discipline approach is something everyone can benefit from. It's been a real treat to watch his growth and progress through the years."

— John "J.J." Johnson, Starting Point Forward, NBA World Champion
Seattle SuperSonics '79

"James Donaldson is a 'will do' type of guy. Whatever challenges were placed in front of him, he would quietly tackle them with hard work and tremendous focus. He not only dreamed about success, but worked for it, accomplishing much along the way. Be it on the basketball court, in the realm of business, or in the community, James constantly stands above others and serves as an inspiration to all who know him."

Mark Edwards (James Donaldson's former assistant coach at Washington State University), Head Men's Basketball Coach, Washington University

"*Standing Above the Crowd* should be mandatory reading for every one of our students throughout the country!"

— Frank Reed, author of *In God We Trust: Dollars and Sense*

"*Standing Above the Crowd* is a moving testament of how a caring adult recognized the potential for inspirational leadership in a shy teenager. A must read for adults and young people alike."

— Rosa Franklin, Senate President Pro Tempore,
2005-2010 Washington State Senate

"I remember visits to James' home when he was a very young, chubby boy who was extremely reserved and polite. As he grew rapidly, no one envisioned that one day he would play basketball in the NBA, but it was apparent that character-wise, he would grow as a Christian and one who would always be concerned about the quality of life for all members of our democratic society. This book reflects the character of the man who has captured the hearts of thousands as he pursues worthy goals on behalf of fellow citizens. He indeed "Stands Above the Crowd" in more ways than one."

— Charles Hall, James Donaldson's Relative

"*Standing Above the Crowd* points out that the Sky is the Limit if you put your heart and mind in to it."

— Nancy Jutton, author of *Bye-Bye Boring Bio Action Guide*

"Of all the candidates I've ever known, no one showed up at work every day with more discipline, dedication, and focus on his job. And he never complained once."

— Carl Silverberg, Political Fundraiser and Strategist

"We were proud to induct you into our Hall of Fame because of your achievements in Athletics, Business, and Community. Thank you for your suggestions and guidance as we changed the name to Multi-Ethnic Sports Hall of Fame. A brilliant stroke!"

— Arif Khatib, Founder/President, Multi-Ethnic Sports Hall of Fame

"I first saw James when we were both freshman at Washington State University and he was playing a pick-up game of basketball in the gym. He had difficulty running—let alone playing basketball. But every year, James got better, to the point of excelling at the highest level possible. Physically James stopped growing as a teenager. But as a person, James continues to grow each and every day. Life is not about peaking—it's about becoming a better person every day. We can all learn from observing James."

— Kevin Phelps, Deputy Pierce County Executive

"I have known 'Dukes' before he became 'Dukes' and he never ceased to amaze me with the ease at which he blends into the crowd given his size. I am sure that is because of his soft spirit and the way he comports himself. A true gentleman! Invite him into your life through his written word and see how much better you are for the effort."

— Jim Marsh, Executive Director, Washington State Mentors

"James has declared his commitment toward peace and reconciliation, and this book shows how and why he earned this reputation."

— Herman McKinney, former Director of the Urban Enterprise Center, Greater Seattle Chamber of Commerce

"Both on the court and off, James has brought to the Seattle region a passion for excellence and a willingness to lead. His core values of education, motivation, and teamwork come through in his book and through his enduring example of leadership."

— Phil Bussey, President & CEO, Greater Seattle Chamber of Commerce

"As an individual who spent over forty years of his life coaching and mentoring young individuals, I recommend this book to anyone seeking greater insight into the fundamentals necessary for successfully mentoring our youth. The fundamentals that James Donaldson articulates are relevant and timely. They slice through the clutter and deliver an insightful approach to delivering your best performance."

— George Raveling, former Washington State University Basketball Coach, International Basketball Director

"I've known James since we were both freshmen student athletes at Washington State University in 1975. At the time, I was an aspiring redshirt-football player. I've observed many athletes in all sports, and James, literally and figuratively, stood above them all! Absolutely no one worked harder and was more dedicated at making himself into a world class athlete than James Donaldson. On top of that, James is a world class person, and anyone reading his book, *Standing Above the Crowd*, will be the better for it."

— Jack "Throwin' Samoan" Thompson, former Washington State University and NFL quarterback

"I first met James in 1975. He joined our team at Washington State University as a quiet, introverted person with raw, undeveloped physical size and athletic ability. Through his persistent effort, hard work, and determination, he transformed himself into an NBA All-Star and the tremendous person he is today. On a personal note, we still consider James a family friend, and my sons grew up thinking everyone had a seven-foot NBA center and his dogs to play with. I have the first-hand knowledge that James didn't just write this book; he lives it!

— Marty Giovacchini, Captain, Washington State University Basketball, 1977

"I would like for everyone who reads your book to know about your coming to prayer meeting every Wednesday when you were in town. Your favorite song was "Further Along We'll Know All About it." I also can recall when your father visited from California. You also brought him to prayer meeting. Now what does this say about you? It tells me that you are a child of God who believes in the power of prayer and one who enjoys the fellowship and love of his brothers and sisters in Christ. God Bless You."

— Reverend Phyllis I. Beaumonte, Seattle, WA

"I have known and worked with James Donaldson, a great friend, at Mount Zion Baptist Church for many, many years. He continues to support our youth and adults in our church programs. James is a great example of spreading the love of Jesus Christ in many, many ways."

— Rev. Frank M. Byrdwell Jr., Minister and Organist at Mount Zion Baptist Church, Seattle, WA

"For those of you who've had the pleasure of casual conversation with James Donaldson, you are already aware of why the title of his book, *Standing Above the Crowd*, is so appropriate. His wisdom, judgment, and humor are all front and center in this very uplifting book."

— Tom "Satch" Sanders, eight-time NBA champion with the Boston Celtics, former NBA executive and businessman

"After a memorable NBA career that spanned fourteen seasons, James Donaldson turned his attention to attacking social problems and helping make the world a better place. He does that job with style, grace, kindness, and wisdom. The Puget Sound area is a better place for having James Donaldson as a resident."

— Mike Gastineau, KJR Sports Radio Talk Show Host

"James Donaldson shares a timely and powerful story, vividly illustrating the role personal clarity plays in the achievement of lifelong success. *Standing Above the Crowd* reflects James' legendary example of living a life knowing who you are and where you are going; achieving extraordinary results in athletics, business, and community. *Standing Above the Crowd* is more than a book—it's the way to live a successful life."

— Colin Brine, CPA, consultant, and cofounder of www.becleaily.com

A SUCCESS ROADMAP FOR HIGH ACHIEVEMENT IN SPORTS & LIFE

STANDING ABOVE THE CROWD

*Execute Your
Game Plan to Become the
Best You Can Be*

AVIVA
PUBLISHING
NEW YORK

James "Dukes" Donaldson

NBA All-Star, Entrepreneur, Community Leader

Standing Above the Crowd
Execute Your Game Plan to Become the Best You Can Be

©2011 by James Donaldson

All Rights Reserved. No part of this book may be used or reproduced in any manner whatsoever without the expressed written permission of the author.

Address all inquiries to:
James Donaldson
3213 W. Wheeler St. Suite 162
Seattle, WA. 98199
1-800-745-3161
JamesD@StandingAboveTheCrowd.com
www.StandingAboveTheCrowd.com

ISBN: 978-1-935586-26-5

Library of Congress Control Number: 2011900507

Proofreader: Tyler R. Tichelaar, Ph.D.
Author Photo: Steve Schneider
Cover Design/Interior Layout: Fusion Creative Works, www.fusioncw.com

Printed in the United States of America

For additional copies, visit:
www.StandingAboveTheCrowd.com

TO MY FATHER, JAMES L. DONALDSON II

With great honor, joy, and admiration, this book is dedicated to my father. He is the man who has been a consistent positive influence throughout my life, and the one who dedicated his life to being the provider, protector, positive influence, and constant presence in the lives of all our family despite the challenges, pressures, and demands that were placed upon him during his own journey through this thing we call "life."

In this media frenzy and photo opportunity world we live in, where dads seem almost absent, and so much credit and adulation is given to "Mom," I want to take this moment to say, "Thank you, Dad."

Dad, you'll never know the full extent of what you meant to me throughout my life. I may have grown to be bigger in physical stature than you and even wear a larger shoe size, but I pale in comparison and will never be able to fill your shoes.

You've blazed trails so I'll never have to put in as much effort to travel them as you have. You've overcome challenges and battles I'll never have to face or fight.

I'll never be able to say thank you enough, but I hope that by my being the model of an exemplary life, I make you happy and proud—it's my way of giving back and saying, "Thank You."

Thank you for being you.

Thank you for being the best "you" that you knew how to be.

Thank you for showing, leading, and helping me to be the best me I can be.

Thank you for being there for all of us (especially me).

Love always,

Your son,

James L. Donaldson III

Special Thanks

I would like to thank the following people for their assistance and friendship over the course of my lifetime, all of whom contributed to bringing this book about:

- Rev. Samuel Berry McKinney, Pastor Emeritus, Mount Zion Baptist Church

- Rev. Frank M. Byrdwell, Music Ministry, Associate Pastor, Mount Zion Baptist Church

- Greg Guedel, great friend and running partner

- Rosemary Bennetts, Operations Manager Extraordinaire

- Ray Berry, outstanding neighbor for thirty years

- John Stimac, my nutritional consultant guru

- Cindi Laws, excellent political consultant

- Michael Lai, great role model for success

- Charles Smith, Executive Director of The Legends of Basketball

- Chuck Wright, for being a great friend over the years

- Jack Gardner, for showing me the way

- Tim "Good Lookin'" Johnson, for being a great Christian Brother

- Lonnie Arnold, an outstanding role model for today's youth

- Patrick Snow, one of the best coaches I've ever had

- Sylvia Parker, dear friend and financial advisor

- Colin Brine, wonderful business mentor and entrepreneur

- Lisa Frahm, for stepping up and helping to co-manage The Donaldson Clinic

- Jodi Kuhn, for stepping up and helping to co-manage The Donaldson Clinic

- Charles Hall, one of my favorite relatives and mentors

- Mitty Alonso, my centenarian friend who saves my seat for me at church

- Ida Mae Hawkins, for putting up with sitting next to me at church all these years

- Coach Dick Motta, for having faith in me and bringing me to the Dallas Mavericks

- Rolando Blackman, for being my "book brother" on the long road trips

- Mike "Little Buddy" Keys, for standing up for me and being a good friend

- Laura Vannucci, for being an awesome physical therapist and wonderful friend

- Tyler Tichelaar, editor/proofreader, for helping me across the finish line with my book

- Shiloh Schroeder, book cover and interior designer of my book

Contents

INTRODUCTION

For readers, the title of this book—*Standing Above the Crowd*—might evoke a chuckle or a nod of recognition as they notice that the author is over seven feet tall. But my goal in writing it is to create more than a simple autobiography about my life as a tall man who played in the NBA. My purpose is to share success strategies and life lessons that, if followed, can give *anyone* the opportunity not just to stand *out* from the crowd, but to **Stand Above the Crowd.**

In these pages, I will share experiences I've had throughout my life, including as a twenty-year professional basketball player, as a twenty-year owner of a small business, a community leader, and my run for elected office in my hometown of Seattle, Washington.

I take the approach that "Anyone can succeed; you just have to try and apply yourself." How many times have you found yourself wanting to take advantage of an opportunity that's right in front of you, only to talk yourself out of it because you didn't think you were up to the task? I'm here to tell you that all successful people have the same thoughts, fears, and apprehensions, yet the successful ones continue to forge ahead anyway. Successful people are not afraid to try and sometimes come up short. Successful people don't always bat 1,000. Successful people have many failures you never hear about before you finally learn of the success that brings them to our attention.

An old Yoruba proverb says, "Your failures in life come from not realizing your nearness to success when you give up." Wow! Think of it. How close to success you probably really are when you give up on chasing and achieving your dreams!

You don't need to be a self-starter and a self-motivated person like myself in order to **Stand Above the Crowd**. All you really need is a vision, passion, the willingness to sacrifice short-term gain for your long-term goals, a belief in yourself and your talents, and then a "stick-to-it" attitude that keeps your eyes on the prize.

One thing you have to remember is that we are all essentially the same. We come into this world bald, wrinkled, and toothless, and when we exit this world, we are bald, wrinkled, and toothless again (well, most of us, anyway!). So what determines our success is how we live our life between Point A, when we enter, and Point B, when we exit.

How do you want to live your life? How do you want to **Stand Above the Crowd**? What kind of meaning and significance do you want your life to have?

My wish is that *Standing Above the Crowd* will help you rise above life's dramas, traumas, pettiness, negativity, and dozens of more situational issues that tend to keep us down and hold us back from achieving our dreams and fulfilling our potential.

I'm a firm believer that we are placed on this earth to be the best we can be. If you're a person of faith like I am, you'll even see that in Scripture, Jesus Christ says He has "come to give life and to give it abundantly." Isn't that beautiful? We all deserve an abundant life, and we can achieve so much more than we have, but many times we find a way to sabotage ourselves and fall far short of our potential.

When I tell people my book is titled, *Standing Above the Crowd,* the first response tends to be, as they look up at me in awe of my physical stature and height, "Well, that's easy for you to say. You're already above the crowd." I quickly respond, "Maybe the title should have been, *Standing Above the Crowd…without being seven feet tall.*" I've had fun with the title, and I have fun with everyone who talks about it with me. But I don't want the message to get lost. I want to encourage people—especially younger readers—to **Stand Above the Crowd**, without having to resort to outrageous tactics that can be embarrassing or damaging to their reputations. After all, there's a huge difference between being "famous" and "infamous." Both get you a lot of attention, but one is a positive thing, and the other quite the opposite.

In these pages, you'll read stories about people I've worked with along the way who had tons more talent than I have, much more physical ability than I could ever wish for, and were way smarter than I could ever hope to be, but I was able to compete alongside them because of what I call my "3-D Approach."

The 3-D Approach is as simple as remembering these three things and applying them to everything you do:

- Desire

- Dedication

- Discipline

I also write about "making an agreement with yourself," aimed especially at young people, to stay away from behaviors or activities that will most likely take you off that road to success.

You'll also hear about the lessons I learned from some of my favorite coaches, such as, "If It's to Be, It's Up to Me" and "Never Be Satisfied."

It can't get much simpler than that, but for whatever reason, many of us find ourselves coming up a little short (no pun intended).

Standing Above the Crowd is jam-packed full of success strategies I've used throughout my life in the areas of athletics, business, and community. All are very straightforward and easy enough for anyone to implement.

Included is helpful advice from the team of wonderful people I've surrounded myself with throughout the years. I've always believed in a team concept approach because we truly can't do it alone. The successes I've had in sports, business, and community involvement have all been because of principles I've learned from many people during my journey.

To borrow a popular phrase, with this book I've attempted to "pay it forward" to you, the reader.

Happy reading!

James Donaldson

Chapter 1

LEADERSHIP—
MAYBE IT'S YOUR TURN

The mark of a good leader is not how many followers he has,
but how many other leaders he creates.
— Author Unknown

When we think of leadership, we perhaps think of such great leaders as President George Washington at Valley Forge; Indira Gandhi, the first female Prime Minister of India; and President John F. Kennedy, with his famous call to action: "Ask not what your country can do for you; ask what you can do for your country."

When *you* think of leadership, what images come to mind? They may depend on your generation, your gender, your culture, or even the neighborhood and household of your childhood.

Leadership is much more than someone stepping forward. After the attempted assassination of President Ronald Reagan and before Vice President George H.W. Bush had arrived back at the White House, the controversial Secretary of State, Alexander Haig, declared, "As of now, I am in control here in the White House." True, it was a time of crisis on a national scale, but many thought this was clearly the action of a power-hungry man. I'm sure Mr. Haig was very much a leader in his own right, but that image has remained etched in our minds.

I've been fortunate through the years to have worked with many admirable leaders. Through athletics, I've been around coaches, team captains, Players Association leaders—leaders off the court, in the locker room, and on the team bus.

A leader isn't always a star people can see from miles away. Many times, a leader is out there doing the "grunt work" and leading by example. A leader gets the respect of many people, even though those people might not express their respect at the time. Most of us know someone like that, someone we respect, someone we can count on, someone we know will be there in a time of need. It's someone we can trust when we need stability, credibility, and wisdom to help us through a tight situation.

When I think of leaders, one person who comes to mind is The Donaldson Clinic's operations manager, Rosemary Bennetts; she stepped up and took on a leadership role as the organization grew. While I may be the founder of The Donaldson Clinic, Rosemary has been with us from Day One. When I decided to turn the mantle of leadership over to someone else, Rosemary suggested that I give the opportunity to her and a couple of other people who had been there for a while. I took her up on it, and she has provided flawless leadership ever since. Rosemary has even groomed a couple of co-managers to work alongside her. That's true leadership!

I have found myself in a leadership role many times. When I was about ten years old, my dad was going off to a continuing education course in Indianapolis. He leaned over to me and told me that I was going to be the "man of the house" while he was away. He wanted me to look out for my mother and my siblings. I can't explain the sense of pride it instilled in me to have my dad trust and empower me to look after things while he was away. Of course, being so young, I didn't know the first thing about leadership, but his confidence in me went a long way in helping me to become comfortable with leadership—no matter what the situation.

I think I did a decent job of being the man of the house while my dad was away. The house was still standing and my brothers and I hadn't beaten the living daylights out of each other! Most remarkable of all, we managed to get most of our chores done before he walked through the door. So, even at a young age, I felt comfortable when called upon to be a leader.

Another experience of being a leader took place when, as a youngster, I took on the responsibility of teaching Sunday School classes at church. My parents made sure we grew up in the church, so Sunday mornings always included Sunday School and church service. People used to say I had a "drug habit" in those early years, because I was "drug" to Sunday School, then "drug" to church service, and then "drug" to a senior citizens' home after church so we could visit the sick and shut-ins. I became quite a scholar through attending Sunday School every week and reading the Bible cover-to-cover numerous times. When I was about twelve, some of the older Sunday School teachers asked me to take over the class for the third-graders. So there I was, not much older than they, reading lessons and Scripture to a group of eight-year-olds. For whatever reason, people have continually asked me to take on leadership responsibilities, and over the years, I have welcomed those opportunities.

It wasn't long before I became a child in a man's body. At about the age of twelve, I hit six feet tall. My dad is 6'3" and wears a size 12 shoe. I think because I have been bigger and taller than my peers for virtually all my life, people have always looked upon me as a leader, if only because I was easy to pick out in any crowd. I wasn't the type of kid who really enjoyed attention. As a matter-of-fact, I'd rather be working behind the scenes than being out front getting attention any day. But as the years passed, I became accustomed to grown-ups asking me to take on my share of responsibility, and then some. Of course, it was up to me not to fumble away those opportunities and to show those who entrusted me with leadership that I could be trusted.

Just about anyone can be a leader, but it does take confidence (something everyone can work at) and being knowledgeable in the given subject matter. I was as shy and introverted as they come when I was growing up, but I loved learning and loved paying attention to things that needed to be done. So when I was called upon to take the lead on something (if it were something I was interested in doing), I usually rose to the occasion. Many times, however, I turned down the opportunity to take the lead because I was working behind the scenes to encourage other people to take on the roles to build their confidence and leadership skills. A leader can be just as effective from the front, the middle, or behind—as long as the rest of the group knows you are committed to achieving the project's goals.

I encourage everyone to take a turn at being a leader. You have it within you to be a leader. You just have to tap into your inherent leadership skills and put them to use. The first few times you take on a leadership role, it will take some nerve and courage. But once you get the hang of it, it starts to become second nature. Try little things at first, such as taking the lead among a group of friends with whom you feel comfortable. Maybe take the lead on a project your group has always wanted to do. Then move up to bigger projects and responsibilities. You'll be amazed by how quickly your confidence grows when it comes to assuming a leadership role.

How do you handle leadership opportunities when they come your way? How strong is your ability to work as part of a team?

Public speaking is said to be everyone's number one fear. If it's not the number one fear, I'd say it's definitely in the top two or three for most people. I'm so glad that when I was a freshman at WSU, one of my basketball coaches encouraged me to take a public speaking class. I did not want to take the class, and I didn't do that well in it, but it paved the way for me to feel comfortable when I speak in public. I had to get up in front of the class to speak. My eyes always wandered off far to the left or right, looking out a window instead of looking at the class. It was painfully hilarious at times, and I don't know if I ever became totally comfortable with it, but it helped me become more comfortable with it as time went on.

Today, I look forward to public speaking. I find it fun to be in front of people and say something with a little humor to make them laugh and to make a connection with them. I've received a lot of speaking tips over the years such as to picture everyone in the audience as naked, mix up your subject matter with humor to keep everyone in a lighthearted mood, don't take yourself too seriously, and have moments in your talk where you poke fun at yourself. I like telling the audiences I speak to that from my vantage point of being over seven feet tall "I can see a lot of combed over bald spots on the guys and plenty of cleavage on the women." That gets them nervously making adjustments to their hair and blouses in a hurry!

My point in this chapter is that you may not feel like you're a naturally born leader, but you have the ability to become a leader. If called upon, you would surprise yourself with what you could do. So, get over your fear of public speaking, being a leader, and taking charge. You ought to take your turn at being a leader.

My favorite all-time coach was New York Knicks Coach Pat Riley. He had a way of supercharging us in the locker room before every game with all kinds of motivational and inspirational tactics. He made us feel like we were going into combat in an all-out war during every game of that eighty-two game NBA season. We'd holler in the hallways, chest bump, and pound on each other on the way out to the basketball court. The players, coaches, trainers, and even the ball boys got caught up in the contagious enthusiasm created by Coach Riley's pep talks.

Now, I'm not an overly emotional guy, but I was seriously enthused and motivated to go out and do my best every day I played for Coach Riley. Plus, I was on a very talented and competitive team, even though I knew—for one of the first times in my career—I wasn't going to break into the starting lineup. I had All-Star and NBA Hall of Famer Patrick Ewing ahead of me, and several younger guys nipping at my heels, but it was still great to play with them and to be part of an enthusiastic team that went to the seventh game of the 1992 Eastern Conference Finals.

POLITICS

Politics is an area most people tend to stay away from until something motivates them to get involved. If there's any area where we need good leaders, it's in politics.

Leaders train themselves to represent people who follow and depend on them for their advice, direction, and motivation. In politics, you represent constituent groups of every shape, creed, and color. All of those people depend on you to do something about their "issues."

When I first got involved in politics, I was amazed at how emotional and personal politics can be. I thought sports generated a lot of emotion and passion, but it was nothing compared to politics. That's because politics are personal and people care a great deal about issues that pertain to them. An issue can be something as simple as having the garbage picked up on a regular basis or being allowed to cut down a tree on a lot when the city says you cannot. Yes, politics are very personal, especially when the issues hit close to home.

If you're a candidate on the political trail, you have to be up on all the issues pertaining to your city, region, or state. I found that most people follow only two or three political issues and don't know much about the rest. That's because they usually feel that the other issues don't pertain to them. A good candidate on the political trail knows how to shift gears and answer questions from a variety of constituents.

The first person I saw get involved personally with the political process was my friend Ida Ballasiotes in the early 1990s. I had been friends with Ida's family since the late 1970s when I was a student at Washington State University. Ida's daughter Diane was a dear friend of mine. In 1987, Diane met an untimely and tragic death when an early release parolee murdered her in a downtown Seattle parking garage and then disposed of her body, which wasn't discovered for several days. Losing such a close friend was one of the saddest things I've ever experienced.

Diane's death motivated Ida to get involved in the political process. She served as a state legislator from 1992-2002. Ida got involved so she could make a difference and change the rules pertaining to the early release of dangerous prison parolees.

That's what leadership is all about. It's when you choose to make a difference, no matter who you are, because it matters to you—and to your community.

Being a leader isn't always a cakewalk. In fact, it's far from it. It takes a strong personality, thick skin, the ability to listen to others, and the ability to create a vision and inspire hope.

If you look at your life right now, you'll find that you already play various leadership roles. If you're an older sibling, most likely you're a leader. If you're a parent, you're a leader. If you're part of a team, you're probably a leader on the team in some capacity. If you're a teacher, mentor, coach, tutor, babysitter, neighborhood watchdog, you're a leader. People depend on you. That in itself elevates you to leadership. You can embrace leadership and the opportunities it brings, or you can shy away from it, and become a leader by default. **Stand Above the Crowd** and be the best leader you can be, even if it's temporary.

After you've had a try at leadership a time or two, you'll most likely start to feel more comfortable with taking a leadership role. Even if it's "holding things together until your leader gets back," you're still demonstrating leadership.

My advice: Embrace the role. When you're a leader, people will look to you to take charge, and they will respect you for the leadership you provide. They will come to count on you because they know you'll come through when it counts most. They'll know you are trustworthy; they'll know you are someone who will stand up to adversity and not run from it. They'll also know you're someone who will be there through thick or thin.

Maybe it's your turn. So, the next time you have an opportunity to be a leader, step forward and **Stand Above the Crowd**. Young people, the next time your teacher counts on you "to keep an eye on things" or to help with chores around the classroom, accept the challenge. Successful people differentiate themselves by accepting a challenge. There will be plenty of time to fall back into the middle of the pack from time to time, but as you get a taste of what leadership is all about, you'll want to be out in front of the pack as a leader rather than a follower.

Chapter 2

DOING IT IN 3-D

Most of us serve our ideals by fits and starts.
The person who makes a success of living is the one who sees
his goal steadily and aims for it unswervingly. That is dedication.
— Cecil B. De Mille

People tend to think that successful people have a magic formula where they snap their fingers and—poof!—everything comes to them without having to work for it. It's as if fame and fortune just happens. I'm here to tell you that's far from the truth. Most of us are familiar with the moral of one of *Aesop's Fables*, "The Hare and the Tortoise": "The race is not won necessarily by the swift or the strong, but by those who persevere." We've also heard that attitude is everything. Yet, even with those time-worn sentiments, people still want to believe that it takes something special and a special person to be successful.

As you get to know me better through this book, you will realize that I'm a simple guy who likes simple solutions. I came up with the 3-D concept years ago when I was playing around with a couple of keywords for a speech I was preparing to give to young people. I wanted to use my last name, Donaldson, in the speech so it would be memorable, but I thought, "There's nothing catchy to play off with my name." Then it came to me—I *could* play off the letter D. And right away, I came up with three keywords that begin with D. As a matter of fact, I put them into a concept we're all familiar with since we are used to seeing things as one-dimensional, two-dimensional, or three-dimensional. Just look around and you can see how many different angles and dimensions there are to just about everything we observe. So I said to myself, why not? Let's do it in 3-D!

My three D's are **D**esire, **D**edication, and **D**iscipline. After having the right attitude, and the persistence to "keep on keeping on," these three keywords are at the top of what it takes to be successful.

DESIRE

Let's look at the first word: Desire. Most of us desire all kinds of wonderful things out of life, but many times our desires end up being just dreams or fantasies instead of reality. Why is that? Desire by itself isn't enough. Desire by itself is nothing more than a wish or a dream. Those aren't going to get you far in life. Wishes and dreams may make you feel better; they might even excite you and give you something to share with your friends and family. But guess what? After hearing your excited raves about your latest dream or fantasy, even family and friends will say (behind your back) that you're nothing more than a dreamer.

We live in a results-oriented world. People want solutions, and they want their problems fixed ASAP. Most people grow tired of listening to someone else's dreams, especially when it remains nothing more than a dream. Dreams are great. We encourage them in youngsters. They need to have dreams. They need to exercise their vivid imaginations because they don't have the skills or life experiences needed to help them channel and form their dreams into reality. Then, once a person becomes older and has had several experiences with life's challenges, it's time to move beyond dreams and start doing something with your life.

I saw plenty of dreaming in NBA training camps before the season began. So many athletes came to training camp with high hopes of becoming NBA players. I've never seen so many grown men cry as I did during those camps when their dreams were snuffed out and they realized they weren't going to make it. Many athletes are so unprepared for the sudden shock of reality that they spend years trying to regain their footing and to find something they can feel comfortable and confident about, just as they did with their NBA dreams.

As a young player with the Seattle SuperSonics, I witnessed a fellow player I'd befriended going through having his dreams dashed during training camp. He was from a small college in Kentucky and had outstanding college statistics. He had a wife and kids, and his whole dream was to make it into the NBA. I only had one year of NBA experience under my belt, but to the guys who had never been there at all, I was an experienced veteran. They sat in amazement as I shared stories of my NBA experience. When my friend got cut and didn't make the team, he broke down in tears right in front of me. He realized his dream was over and that he'd soon head back to "real life" with his family. He was very distraught and in a bad frame of mind when he packed up and said his goodbyes. I'm not sure whatever became of him, but he seemed to have a good head on his shoulders, so I hope he found something and somewhere else to channel his focus and energy.

It's good to dream, it's good to have passion, and it's good to have desires and fantasies, but remember—all those things require follow-up if you seriously want to embark upon your journey of success. When I meet young people who have dreams and goals, I listen to them and encourage them to fulfill those dreams and goals. Our great country would never have been discovered if people hadn't desired to see what was beyond the horizon when others thought the world was flat. Many of the social changes that needed to take place in our country would have never been attempted if someone hadn't dreamed and desired to make things different for everyone—and to put in the effort to make a difference.

If you have a desire, follow it and see where it leads you. Develop that passion that will lead you through the obstacles you'll encounter while going after your desire. That's the way change comes about, but first you must have a desire for change.

DEDICATION

After you've developed a desire to do something different with your life and to pursue a dream, you need to figure out a way to follow through with your desire. Just as with the tortoise in the fable, here is where **D**edication comes in.

Dedication means making sure your desire is a priority in your life. It means that you are willing to put in the time, effort, energy, and resources to make it come true. It means sacrificing time you once spent with your friends, watching TV, surfing the net, traveling, taking vacations, and giving up or limiting anything else that could get in the way of making your desire and dream become a reality.

I remember my days at Washington State University. I'd made a commitment to be the best student athlete I could be. Back then, in the late 1970s and early 1980s, WSU was ranked as one of the top ten schools for drinking and partying. There wasn't a weekend when carloads of students didn't head out to the bars, taverns, and nightclubs either near campus or just a short drive across the state line into Idaho. My friends asked me repeatedly to go with them, but my answer was always, "No, I have to stay home and do my homework," or "No, I need to get some rest so I can get up early tomorrow morning for practice and training." I chose to take that path because I was dedicated to being the best I could be.

Sure, some people called me "square," not hip, uncool, you name it, but I stuck to my guns and told myself that all of those good times and parties would be there for me to enjoy once I reached my goal. It may seem like a miracle that I was able to go to such a big drinking and partying school and never once taste alcohol, but I had made that promise to myself while I was growing up in Sacramento and dreaming about becoming a professional basketball player, so it was a relatively easy promise to keep, even under tremendous peer pressure.

Being able to resist overwhelming peer pressure to make the right choices for yourself is part of what it means to **Stand Above the Crowd**. It means making the right choices, even when your friends make fun of you and tease you about not being cool. It means being happy with yourself, knowing you made the right choices; it means not having to pay the consequences that some of your friends will pay because of the poor choices they made.

After a while, your friends will see that you're a person with conviction, strong values, and morals. You'll find that many of your friends will become protective of you, telling your pressuring peers to back off because you don't drink or you don't sleep around. Either they're becoming protective of you, or they're getting tired of hearing you say, "No" every time they ask you to do something. The ones who don't understand will drift away and aren't really your friends anyway. In either case, the situation is good because it helps you to stick to your convictions.

You'll actually garner a certain measure of respect from your peers if you're able to stick to your convictions. People find it easier to pull you down to their level (into their drama, trauma, and issues) than to elevate themselves to where you are. That's human nature, so don't feel bad about it or let people make you feel bad about what you're doing. Don't let them do that to you! Remember, you have "the power," and as long as you stick to your dreams, you hang onto "the power." Hopefully, one day your friends will find their own power and elevate their games to your level.

DISCIPLINE

Discipline is the third leg of what it takes to be successful and stay on the road to success. Desire fuels your passion and gives you the energy to pursue your goal. Dedication helps you start prioritizing your activities surrounding your desire so it becomes more than just a dream. Discipline keeps you "keeping on" during even the most challenging times.

It takes tremendous discipline not only to *become* successful, but also to *stay* successful. It's one thing to climb the mountain; it's another to figure out how to stay on top of the mountain for any length of time.

You hear stories from time to time of people who make it to the summit of a great mountain, only to succumb to its extreme temperatures and environment because they weren't prepared or because they just ran out of what it takes to survive in those extreme conditions. Don't let that happen to you! Make sure you realize not only what it takes to be successful, but also understand the tremendous challenges, sacrifices, and demands you'll face if you're going to stay at the top.

As a professional athlete, I knew I was embarking upon a demanding career that would take almost all of my focus, energy, and time if I were going to be good at it. The average NBA career is only three years, but I went into professional basketball telling myself that I wanted to be the first NBA player to play until he was forty years of age. Now, I didn't quite play all my professional basketball years in the NBA (fourteen were in the NBA), but I played professional basketball until I was forty-two. By the time I reached that goal, two or three other guys had gotten there first. We all played in the same era and played against each other on many occasions.

I knew I could never give the kind of attention and sacrifice necessary to be successful at an NBA career while at the same time giving that same attention and sacrifice to having a family—one or the other of them would end up being seriously compromised. So I did what I thought was smart and the right thing for me; I pursued my NBA career with all the gusto and determination I had. I chose to delay any possibility of getting married and having children until after my NBA career was over.

Sometimes a window of opportunity is open only for a short time, and you just don't know how long it will stay open. Although my goal to play until I was forty was unusual, it didn't seem like such a far-fetched idea, especially since bigger guys tend to play a lot longer than smaller players in the NBA.

Now that my professional basketball career has ended, I've turned to pursuing the possibility of having a wife and children, a pursuit that has turned out to be more challenging than I thought it would be! As with anything, it takes a 3-D approach to make it happen and a 3-D approach by both people to make it work. I just have to make it my number one objective someday soon and move it up on my priority list in order to make it happen. Of course, individual goals are a lot easier to accomplish than goals that require an intimate relationship between two people. I'll keep working on it; don't worry!

Discipline comes relatively easily for me. I think that's because I was able to lay that foundation, or that foundation was laid for me, at a relatively early age. My father was in the U.S. Air Force for twenty years, so he instilled discipline in me when I was still very young. I grew up knowing the value of hard work, patience, and persistence. I fear many of our young people today are missing out on those fundamental aspects of life. As a kid, of course, I didn't understand the reasons behind the strictness and discipline my father and mother put us through. Looking back on it now, I'm glad that they instilled such values in me. My upbringing prepared me to take on just about any of life's challenges. My early years were the start of the 3-D approach.

I encourage all parents to discipline their children on a consistent and constant basis. Discipline doesn't have to be mean-spirited, but it does need to be consistent. We know kids are great at playing one parent against the other; parents and role models need to be aware of that and not let it happen. Parents need to be more communicative with their children than they were when I was growing up. Back then, it was enough for my parents to tell me what I needed to do with very little if any explanation. Today, not necessarily because they are any smarter, children require and expect to be communicated with at a level they can understand. They need to know why you are asking them to do certain things. I'll admit: I don't get it! I guess it's the "old school" in me. But I am willing to continue growing with the changes, and I know that flexibility keeps me on top of things.

As a child, I had many different experiences that still help me stay disciplined and focused. First, we always went to church, and church teaches you discipline. It's what being a disciple is about. Jesus surrounded himself with disciplined followers—disciples—and He wants all of us to go out and spread His wonderful message.

I was also involved with scouting. I moved up through the ranks from Cub Scout to Webelo, and stopped just short of becoming a Boy Scout. Scouting taught me a lot about being disciplined, staying positive, and pursuing my goals. It taught me about sharing and giving back to my community. It taught me about treating others fairly and being a good role model. Scouting has a lot to offer young boys and girls, and it's a great way to build a positive foundation for our young people.

Getting good grades in school requires a lot of discipline. Students come home day after day with a homework assignment to be completed for the next day. I'm glad to see it's still expected from most school-age kids. I encourage parents and role models to support teachers by making sure their kids complete their homework assignments in a timely manner. We need to encourage our young students to strive to be the best they can be.

That's what "Doing it in 3-D" is all about. Once you have a *desire* to do something, it becomes more than just a dream or fantasy. Then it moves up your priority list so it becomes something to which you *dedicate* the vast amount of your time, effort, and resources. Then you stay *disciplined* at it, day after day, week after week, and year after year. That's the formula for success! And guess what? It's something every one of us can do. There's not a lot of razzle-dazzle about it, but there is a lot of "stick-to-it-tiveness" if you're going to make it happen. It's about being patient, doing whatever it takes to make it happen, and hanging in there.

Chapter 3

GOAL SETTING
AIM HIGH, SHOOT STRAIGHT

Most of us serve our ideals by fits and starts.
The person who makes a success of living is the one who sees
his goal steadily and aims for it unswervingly. That is dedication.
— Cecil B. De Mille

I have always been a goal-setting kind of guy. One thing I emphasize when I speak to young people is how important it is for them to set goals before they graduate from high school. First, I try to help them envision graduating from high school, and then to envision themselves focusing on and eventually succeeding at their goals.

Goal setting is important, but it also can be fun. When you're passionate about a goal, you have a reason to get up in the morning. When you know that the day ahead of you will be filled with wonderful opportunities, you can see yourself making progress as you march toward your goals.

Our goals may not always bring about the results we initially envisioned, but they will still get us closer to what we want and we will have wonderful opportunities along the way. For example, remember my goal when I was a rookie in the NBA to play until I was forty years old? Back in 1980 when I set that goal, no one played until that age. With the average NBA career being only three years, few NBA players could foresee themselves playing past their mid-thirties, and perhaps as a result of not thinking it was likely to happen, few of the players ever did play past that age. It's a funny thing, but when the mind starts telling you certain things (negative or positive), your body has a way of just following along. So if you're in your mid-thirties and tell yourself you're old and washed up, you probably will be.

I ended up playing professional basketball until I was forty-two years old. I played fourteen years in the NBA, and six years overseas. That's a twenty-year professional basketball career. It wasn't exactly the way I thought I would spend the last six years of my career. At the time, I didn't appreciate the experience my time overseas would give me. My ego and pride kept me wishing I had played all twenty years in the NBA. But now when I reflect upon the wonderful opportunities basketball gave me, I'm grateful I spent six years traveling through Europe and other countries.

During those years of playing ball overseas, I learned to speak Spanish, Italian, and Greek darn near fluently as I constantly found myself in small gatherings of people who barely spoke a word of English. I was able to learn those languages because I was open to getting to know the people in other countries and learning about their history and culture. Many times groups of schoolchildren and teenagers would meet me at local coffee shops and spend hours teaching me their languages. In exchange, all they wanted was to have an American friend and to improve their English.

Many of my teammates (especially the Americans), by contrast, would lock themselves away in their apartments rather than engage with the native people. I recall vividly how so often the American players would head straight to the nearest American fast food joint and gorge themselves on junk food instead of taking time to enjoy and understand the various countries we were temporarily calling home. I would hear loud American music thumping through the walls of their apartments as they isolated themselves from the opportunities provided by experiencing a different culture. I felt it was their loss.

So, while my goals ended up not coming to fruition exactly as I had planned, I took advantage of the opportunities that resulted, and I had wonderful and memorable experiences as a result.

Today, a handful of NBA players have played past their fortieth birthdays. The bigger guys can usually play for a longer time because they don't rely on speed as much as the smaller guys do. So when the little bit of speed and quickness we do have starts to wane, it's no big deal, especially if we've learned to adjust our game throughout the years. Similarly, with goals, you may have to adjust your goals now and then, but that doesn't mean you give up on them; you simply adjust them so you still achieve what you basically want.

BUSINESS

Goal setting is important in everything you do. If you don't have a goal, it's going to be difficult to maintain focus and measure your progress.

After years of being involved in athletics, I wanted to start my own physical therapy business to help athletes and others who needed physical or massage therapy. When I began The Donaldson Clinic in 1990, I had several goals I wanted to accomplish. Of course, the main goal was to create and establish a successful business. The average new small business in the United States fails within two years. I knew I didn't want "average" to apply to me, so I worked hard to make sure we would surpass average and keep on going.

My next goal with The Donaldson Clinic was to grow the business to the point where we would have multiple locations throughout the greater Puget Sound area. I and my staff were able to accomplish that after I fully retired from professional basketball and had the time to make that happen. After we established our original location in Mill Creek, we established a satellite clinic in the city of Kirkland in 1994, followed shortly by clinics in Cashmere, Tacoma, Seattle, and Mukilteo. I achieved my goal of building and growing my business because I created the vision, set goals, implanted a strategy, and executed a plan. We can all succeed with our goals; we just need to make sure we know what we need to do to achieve them and then execute a plan to make it happen.

ATHLETICS

Approximately 250,000 high school seniors play football every year in the United States. Out of that number, statistics show that about 5.8 percent of them will go on to play college football, and of those who play football in college, only 8 in 10,000 will go on to play in the NFL. That's an awfully low number and very high odds!

With basketball, the number of young people playing ball is even more competitive. According to the NCAA, less than 1 in 35 high school senior boys playing high school basketball will go on to play at an NCAA member institution, and only 1 in 75 of them will land an NBA contract. Those are the odds and numbers. I don't present them to deter you if playing professional ball is your goal. My point is that you will have to work at it to achieve that goal.

Whatever your goal is, be realistic about your abilities and the odds and make sure you have what it takes to reach that goal, or adjust your goal until you find one that will challenge you yet you still believe you can obtain. Work incredibly hard and diligently toward reaching your goals. Do everything it takes to be one of the best in your field. Find a mentor to help you navigate your way, and keep your eyes and mind open to opportunities. Sometimes you may have to settle for less than your ultimate goal, but sometimes, that goal can be achieved later. For example, before I went on to play for the NBA, I ended up playing in Italy for a year, but that year helped me to refine my skills so I could be a better player later when the opportunity opened up for me to play in the NBA.

In closing, here are some basic steps to make your goals effective:

Write it down. Then go back and read it again and again to remind yourself of it; your mind will then become focused on ways to bring it about. Post it where you can see it frequently, like a mirror, a desk, or the dashboard of your car.

1. Create a plan to execute the goal.

2. Set measurable goals. Goals are accomplished one step at a time. Set short-term goals to get you to your long-term goals.

3. Create deadlines for achieving your goals. Review the deadlines frequently, adjusting them as needed but striving to meet the deadlines and goals within reasonable timeframes.

4. Celebrate when you achieve your goals. Reward yourself or at least pat yourself on the back. By taking time to appreciate yourself for whatever you achieve, no matter how big or small, you will build confidence in yourself and prepare yourself to go on to achieving even bigger success.

The Future is a Big Adventure[1]

Sooner or later, those who win are those who think they can.

The cards you're dealt in life are less important than the way you play them.
Every day you face a new deck and new cards.

Carve out a niche for yourself in your imagined future.
Begin immediately to view yourself as successful.
To achieve your goal in life, you need to project your end result.

Focus on your future, not your past.
Prepare for your future; don't live in the past.
Relish your good memories and use any bad ones as lessons in life.

Think of the elation, the satisfaction, and the joy you'll feel when you've achieved your objective. Carry these ecstatic feelings with you every day to keep your desired goals in view.

Success is waiting for you.

---

1 ©2006 by Max Steingart. Reproduce freely but maintain © notice

Chapter 4

MENTORING
SOMEONE IS LOOKING UP TO YOU

A life isn't significant except for its impact on other lives.
— Jackie Robinson

If you take some time to look back over your life, you'll recall numerous people who have been a positive influence on your life in one capacity or another. Anyone who has had that kind of effect on another is worthy to be called a "mentor."

Being coached by Hall of Fame great **Lenny Wilkens** was one of the most fortunate things that could have happened to me upon starting my NBA career. He was definitely one of my biggest mentors.

I was drafted by the Seattle SuperSonics in 1979, the year of its NBA world championship. As I had taken a detour to Italy for a year, I didn't join the Sonics until the 1980 season. The team was still in its prime then since it was manned with NBA championship-caliber players. My teammates were "Downtown" Freddie Brown, John "JJ" Johnson, Jack Sikma, Lonnie Shelton, and Gus Williams. That was a great team to break in with!

Coach Wilkens was a good mentor for me because he treated me like the young professional I was. He allowed me to mature into a *bona fide* NBA player, while at the same time having high expectations for me. That's what great mentors do: They play to your strengths and minimize your weaknesses.

One of Coach Wilkens' strengths was his ability to delegate responsibility to other leaders on the team. He would oversee from the sidelines while my more experienced teammates, such as Fred Brown and John Johnson, would work on the basic fundamentals I needed to perfect if I were going to succeed as an NBA player. He expected us always to be professionals and to conduct ourselves as such. I was allowed to flourish under his coaching, while at the same time not have unrealistic expectations placed upon me.

Wilkens wasn't a "jump in your face and cuss you out" kind of a coach or mentor, and I appreciated that. He was always very cool and seemingly unrattled by the rigors of an NBA season. That showed me early on that you have to keep a cool head about yourself while pushing yourself to be the very best you can be.

Mentors of course come in all shapes, sizes, ages, genders, and with a variety of different personalities and backgrounds. As long as a mentor is a positive influence in your life, it really doesn't matter where he or she comes from or looks like.

When it comes to mentoring young children, teenagers, and young adults, it's best for women to mentor girls and for men to mentor boys as much as possible. When children are at a young age, they are satisfied with getting attention from just about anyone, but as a child matures, many changes occur that are gender-specific in nature, and adolescents feel more comfortable with someone whom they know has personal experience and not just "book knowledge" in what they are experiencing.

Puberty is an awkward time for young people, and along with the physical changes taking place, issues of self-image and being self-conscious can be better dealt with by matching them up with mentors of the same sex. Not that those kinds of things can't be overcome, but for simplicity and comfort, both the mentors and mentees will typically find that connecting with the same gender is best. But whatever sex you are, when it comes right down to it, as long as you provide a positive influence in someone's life, you're a mentor.

Following are some examples of mentors I've had at different stages in my life. I'll discuss them in the order they entered my life.

MY FIRST, AND BEST, MENTOR

I've been blessed over the years with an abundance of mentors. As I look back, I'd have to say my first mentor, of course, was my dad, James Lee Donaldson, Sr. He's had a positive influence on me as far back as I can remember. His military background and training instilled in me at a very young age the concepts of discipline and accountability.

Even though my dad looked every bit the athletic type at 6'3" and 220 pounds, he didn't especially encourage us to participate in sports as we were growing up. His focus was on taking care of and providing for the family. He made sure we had a roof over our heads and meals on the table, no matter what sacrifices he had to make. And no matter how hard I try to convey it, he will probably never understand how much I appreciate everything he has done for me.

My dad spent twenty years in the U.S. Air Force and another twenty with the U.S. Postal Service. I can probably count on one hand the number of days he stayed home because he was tired or ill. He was one of those guys who continued to "keep on keeping on," doing the best job he could do, no matter what obstacles he faced.

My dad grew up in Indianapolis; after being abandoned by his family at an early age, he was taken in and raised by another family in the neighborhood. Growing up in the 1930s, my dad knew and suffered through all the social and racial issues of the day; however, my dad did a tremendous job of not burdening our family with what he had gone through in his past. As a result, I grew up with an objective perspective on the world and derived conclusions based on my own experiences, not my dad's. I wish more parents today followed that example.

My dad belonged to the generation that believed a father's primary responsibility was to provide for his family. When my dad came home from a long day at work, he didn't play with us or take us to the ball field. He did, however, check to make sure we'd done our chores and homework and that we were obedient to our mother. If we were out of line, it wasn't unusual for him to take a strap to us, or as many families did back then, send us into the backyard to select a tree branch that he would use to whip us. I remember going out to the backyard on many occasions to find a branch with leaves on it, hopefully, to cushion the blow. I also would either double- or triple-layer the pants I was wearing, or find a pillow to absorb the blows. That usually worked fairly well, unless I laughed because I thought I was getting away with something. A couple of times, my dad realized that, with all my padding and my carefully chosen branch, I didn't understand his "message." His solution was to have me "un-layer" myself until I was down to my briefs. Then the discipline proceeded. In the end, I always got the message!

I've been blessed with a long succession of mentors in my life, but none matches the effective mentoring/fathering I got from my own dad. He did a good job, not only with me, but with all the kids in our family. He continues to be a fine role model, even now that we're all adults.

My dad and I have grown closer over the years and we talk every Sunday morning as we prepare for our respective church services. I look forward to our conversations, and I treasure every one of them.

BILL, THE CROSSWALK MAN

The next significant mentor I can remember is an elderly man who was a crosswalk guard when I was in grade school. We called him "Bill, the Crosswalk Man." He was there every day before and after school, making sure we got across the busy highway that divided my neighborhood and the path to school. Bill shuffled out to the middle of the street, holding his stop sign in his hand for all oncoming traffic to see, and then he motioned us safely across the street.

Edward Kimball Elementary School was about a one-mile walk from my home in South Sacramento, California. We crossed busy Florin Road, and even though it had a traffic light and a crosswalk, we wouldn't have been safe crossing it without a crosswalk guard's protection. Then, once we made it across Florin Road, we had quite a trek through open fields and a couple of neighborhoods before we made it to school.

Bill, the Crosswalk Man, for whatever reason (maybe because I was taller than the other kids), took a special interest in me. He always tossed some words of wisdom my way every day. I remember he always made sure my shoes were tied, my pants were pulled up, that I didn't splash my way through mud puddles, and that I respected my books and the book bag

I carried. He'd say things like, "Tuck in that shirt, young fella," or, "Tie your shoes so you don't trip," and "How ya doin' in school?" I felt a little special because he'd taken a special interest in me.

I always thought about "Bill, the Crosswalk Man" as I approached that crosswalk going to school. I never knew what he was going to say to me, but I knew it would be something positive. I looked forward to it every day, and I missed it whenever he had a day off.

Mentors can have an impact on you in many ways. "Bill, the Crosswalk Man" helped me feel special, which in turn, helped me to develop a certain sense of self-esteem. You never know what impact you might have on young people. Why, just acknowledging them is an impact in itself. Most of the time, it's a positive impact and something the young person will always remember.

COACH CHUCK CALHOUN

If I had to say which mentor had the most positive and influential impact on me, other than my dad, it would have to be my high school basketball coach, Charles "Chuck" Calhoun. Keep in mind that coaches coach more than just sports; coaches coach business and life skills also.

On my first day of high school, the football coach asked, begged, and pleaded with me to try out for the football team. I told him, "No, I'm not interested." He told me I'd only need to stand on the field with my hands up and block field goals. He jumped around and waved his hands, simulating what it would look like. I again declined.

Over the next few days, the track coach asked me to try out for the track team and perhaps do the shot put or the discus. Just as I'd told the football coach, I told the track coach I wasn't interested.

I'm sure word got around to the basketball coach, Chuck Calhoun, that there was a big kid (I was about 6'8" at the time), a freshman on campus, who didn't want to play sports. However it happened, once Coach Calhoun took an interest in me, the football and track coaches never bothered me again.

When I first encountered Coach Calhoun, he, of course, asked me to try out for the basketball team. I told him I wasn't interested. I had played some occasional pick-up basketball prior to that, but I'd never played organized basketball, much less been on a real team, up to that point.

One of the reasons I had no interest in sports when I began high school was because I hadn't been allowed to play baseball when I was eight years old. I was big and tall enough at that age, but I wasn't old enough (you had to be at least ten years old). At eight, I didn't understand why I wasn't allowed to play, but after that, I didn't want to face rejection again, so I stayed away from organized sports. My parents weren't like most sports-crazed parents today who would probably file a lawsuit if their kid weren't allowed to play. My parents (and I) didn't make a big deal out of it. We went on our way, but the situation did have a lasting impact on me.

When my sophomore year rolled around, Coach Calhoun asked me again to try out for the basketball team. Once again, I told him I wasn't interested. By this time, I'd grown another inch or two, but I was not very athletic. Sure, I was a big and tall kid, but it was probably obvious that I wasn't very confident about being in such a body. I would slink along the walls of the school hallways (as much as a 6'8", 300-pounder can slink!), hoping the kids wouldn't notice me too much. I didn't like attention, and I didn't want anyone to notice how big and tall I was. Not that I really realized how big and tall I was at the time; I just didn't enjoy the attention and commotion. Looking back now, I smile because that was nothing compared to the attention and commotion I cause even now, everywhere I go!

Coach Calhoun tried again at the start of my junior year. This time he had a different strategy. I think by then he had realized what kind of kid I was, so he figured out a new way to get me out on the basketball court. I didn't realize my potential and I didn't believe in myself. I was insecure, uncoordinated, and not comfortable with my size. Before I could say no, Coach Calhoun said he only wanted me to come out and practice with the guys. I wouldn't have to play during the games. I didn't know what that meant, but I decided to give it a try. I learned a lesson then, and have implemented it many times over the years: If you don't try, you'll never know what you can do.

On Coach Calhoun's recommendation, I started running and training for the first time in my life. I had a lot of weight to lose if I were going to become the athlete hidden away inside of me. Every day after practice, I ran three or four miles around the school field. I also started following a more healthy diet (remember, I grew up loving junk food and candy). Over the course of my junior year, I lost nearly 100 pounds and started acquiring the shape of a future athlete. It took someone like Coach Calhoun to realize an athlete was inside me and to figure out how to tap my vast pool of potential. He knew I was a good kid, so if nothing else, I would be willing to listen, be coachable, and stay out of trouble.

Coach Calhoun knew I would probably be frightened at the first sign of anyone intimidating me, or more likely, laughing at me. So he took great strides to cover every window in the gym with newspaper so no one could look in and I could practice with the basketball team without anxiety. We had a good team that year. All the players were better than me, and most of them were older, so I really didn't feel much pressure to prove myself, or even to try to make the team.

After a few weeks of practice, I gradually got the feel for what the game of basketball is all about. Since I'd stayed away from athletics all my life, I had to start from the very beginning of the game. Because of my lack of coordination, I actually had to learn how to walk and chew gum at the same time without tripping over my size-18 feet! I learned how to run and how to jump in a coordinated manner. I did hundreds of tap drills where I jumped up and tapped the rim with both hands. I learned to start handling the basketball and became more comfortable with it. Basics, such as catching the ball, dribbling, and circling it around my head or my waist without fumbling were things I practiced all through my junior year.

I started to feel much more comfortable and my confidence grew as practice continued. After a while, I wasn't in such a hurry to run home to eat, watch TV, and be in the backyard with my pet homing pigeons. I still did those things, just after basketball practice was over.

I didn't play my first official basketball game until I was a senior in high school. I wasn't an outstanding player by any means, but because someone took a special interest in me, I had a newfound confidence in my abilities. Coach Calhoun, who saw the potential deep inside of me way before I even dreamed I had that kind of ability, made it possible for me to be the athlete I am today.

In that first game, I stumbled and bumbled my way to about twenty-five points, fifteen rebounds, and five or six block shots. I don't know how I did that! I never approached those numbers again during the rest of my senior year. I played well enough (double-double in points and rebounds) to attract the attention of college scouts, who were interested in me—not so much for my basketball skills, but for my potential and the fact that I was willing to listen, learn, and be coached.

Young people, if you want to get on that track to success, you must be willing to listen, learn, and be coachable. No matter what your background, no matter your insecurities or issues, no matter what kind of ability you have at the time, don't ever give up on yourself. Be willing to listen and learn.

I owe a great debt of gratitude to Coach Calhoun, who saw me blossom as a student athlete at Washington State University and then through my career with the NBA. Coach Calhoun enjoyed coming to see me play against the Sacramento Kings or the Golden State Warriors when I was in town on a visiting team.

Coach Calhoun has passed away, but his legacy lives on as I continue to tap into my potential and I see and develop the potential within others. Coach Calhoun taught me that no matter where you are in life, if you're willing to listen, learn, and be coachable, then the sky's the limit! Being coachable doesn't necessarily pertain only to sports, but to just about everything in life that requires someone to provide you with strategy and focus so you can achieve your desired end results and full potential. Thanks, Coach Calhoun. I will always remember you!

COACH GEORGE RAVELING

I first met Coach George Raveling after I graduated from high school and took a recruiting trip to Washington State University.

George Raveling became my "second father," someone I needed as a young man sprouting wings and leaving home for the first time. He gave me a sense of self-esteem that grew throughout my collegiate years. I respected him and liked him a lot, too.

Coach Raveling was very much the taskmaster. He rode the team hard. He had a fiery temper and wasn't afraid to show it. I think he saw quickly that I wasn't going to need much handholding, but because several of the other guys required a lot of attention, I got to see his temper firsthand, and it wasn't a pretty sight.

The team always had a "class clown" who could mimic Coach Raveling's ravings to the tee. We'd double over in laughter! Even to this day when I bump into some of my old teammates, someone invariably mimics "The Rave." That brings back some wonderful memories.

College was a crucial time in my life, as it is for any young person leaving home for the first time. Coach Raveling was a great mentor because he held me accountable and helped me to understand the importance of that trait as I matured. On the wall of Coach Raveling's office hung a plaque with his guiding principle: ***If It's to Be, It's Up to Me.*** Anytime an athlete walked in Coach's office, that message was staring him in the face; as a result, that phrase has stuck in my head for many years and become my guiding principle as well.

I owe so much to Coach Raveling. I appreciate him to this day. Every young person could benefit from a mentor like him.

COACH TOM PUGLIESE

I'd say one of the most enjoyable mentoring experiences I have had was with the assistant basketball coach at Washington State University, Tom Pugliese.

Working with Tom was enjoyable not only because I had a great relationship with Tom, but with his family, too. His son, Rorie, became one of my very best friends. I was so infatuated with Tracy, his daughter, that I would have done anything in the world for her. His wife, Joan, became part of the team at The Donaldson Clinic years ago and remains with us to this day.

Although Coach Tom passed away several years ago, his legacy lives on in me in many different ways. I was at his bedside just hours before he left us, and I let his family and him know how much I appreciated him and loved him for being with me through so many memorable years. Coach Tom's family is still as near and dear to me as they were when we first met more than thirty years ago. Tom Pugliese was a wonderful mentor because he too saw tremendous potential in me and pushed me to do my best. I worked closely with him all four of my years as a student athlete at WSU.

Athletes tend to form a closer relationship with the assistant coaches than they do with the head coach. Assistant coaches typically act as intermediaries who can help you communicate better with the head coach, and vice versa. You go to assistant coaches when you want to whine and complain about not being utilized properly or not getting enough play time. You don't dare do that with your head coach unless you're one of the superstar players.

Always keep in mind: coaches are not just coaching the mechanics of a sport; they are guiding us in many life skills that will carry over to every aspect of our lives, life skills that include: accountability, respect, team-work, self-discipline, and self-confidence.

FREDDIE "DOWNTOWN" BROWN AND JOHN "JJ" JOHNSON

My early Sonic teammates Freddie "Downtown" Brown and John "JJ" Johnson were great mentors at the start of my NBA career. As I mentioned earlier, they were key elements of the 1979 Seattle SuperSonics NBA championship team. Both were NBA veterans from "the old-school," and for them it was all about winning. They didn't have time for nonsense, but they didn't mind helping out younger players like me, as long as we were willing to listen and learn.

I still remember how JJ insisted I arrive at practice early and stay late—none of this arriving to practice right at starting time and then bolting out as soon as practice was over. That's not what makes championship players—or successful people. JJ, one of the few people who call me "Jimmy," would always be there waiting for me, and we got to work right away. He was a forerunner to the versatile NBA player who could do just about anything (pass, score, play defense, operate the offense, etc.). He was a small forward, but often the offense originated through him because he had an uncanny way of seeing the plays unfold in front of him and getting the ball to the right people. He also was a terrific defender and didn't hesitate in taking on the opponent's best players. He was one of my best mentors at teaching me toughness and preparing me for the NBA. We spent a good half hour or so before practice working on various post moves as JJ fed the ball to me from various angles and then had me kick the ball out to him while I reposted for better position. We worked on these drills before practice, every day, more times than I can count.

After practice, JJ and Fred put me to work on rebounding drills. Again, JJ would pass the ball in to me, and I'd pass the ball out to Fred, who was spotting up beyond the three-point line. Actually, the three-point line didn't even exist in the NBA until the mid-1980s. Too bad, because then Fred Brown would have had at least 30 percent more points to his credit. During Fred's days, people knew him for his uncanny marksmanship "from way downtown," thus, his nickname.

I took a certain pride in the fact that these two established veterans even made time for me. I looked forward to arriving at practice early so I could work out with JJ, and I was glad to stay late so I could work out with both of them. I chased balls all over the gym as Fred bombed away from "downtown." Ever the practical joker, Fred sometimes seemed to miss on purpose so I'd have to chase the ball up into the bleachers, while at other times, he easily swished ten in a row as if it were nothing. Either way, it gave me a great sense of timing the ball, where it might or might not come off the rim, and getting in position to box out and go for the rebound.

That's what it takes to be successful: Repetition, practice, and an endless pursuit of perfection. I look at a lot of pro athletes today, and many of them don't want to put in the extra time and effort once they make it to the pros. That's a big reason many of them fall far short of their potential. That leads to shortened careers, because eventually, someone will come up behind you who's hungrier than you and won't stop until he gets it, and that means beating you out of your position. I wasn't about to let that happen to me, so I remained a hard worker throughout my whole NBA career.

I'm still good friends with Fred Brown and John Johnson. They both serve as mentors to me, and I never hesitate to pick up the phone to run things by them or to solicit their advice. In a way, I feel like their "little brother" (and they treat me as such it seems), but that's okay. I give them the respect they deserve because I appreciate their keeping me focused on the task at hand even to this day.

CLIFFORD RAY

The mentor who kept me on the straight-and-narrow and helped me become the pro I became was Clifford Ray. Clifford coached me on playing the center position when I was with the Dallas Mavericks (1985-1992), and he and I became close friends and mentor/mentee. Probably more than anyone else, he taught me how to play the pro game. He taught me how to be tough and compete out there. He also helped me understand the responsibilities a center has toward his teammates in looking out for them and protecting them from teams that want to play extra-physical against them. He taught me how to do the little things (like block shots, get tip-ins, hustle all the time, and play defense on anyone who came close to the basket) on the court to help my team win without having the ball in my hands and taking a lot of shots.

Clifford was starting center on the 1975 NBA Championship Golden State Warriors and was a very good player in the league for a long time. So he knew what he was talking about. He mentored not only me, but also the other centers and big guys on the team. He had the unenviable job of watching out for some of our "troubled" players, a thankless job. Clifford was my guy, and we stay in touch, even all these years after we've both hung up our sneakers. Everyone would benefit from having a Clifford Ray on his team!

MENTORS ARE EVERYWHERE

As I mentioned at the beginning of this chapter, mentors come in a variety of forms. They also come along at various stages of our lives to help and join us in our journeys. I have tremendous mentors even now in the fields of business, politics, faith, community involvement, and plain old everyday life.

Rev. Frank M. Byrdwell, Jr. from my Mount Zion Baptist Church home in Seattle is a perfect example. I recall how often he and I have gotten together for lunch over the years. He helped me visualize a Donaldson Clinic location in Central Seattle, close to our church, to serve the neighborhood. He kept that little light of mine shining over the years, and in 2004, we were able to open a clinic there. I even named the aquatic therapy pool after Rev. Byrdwell to show my appreciation for his helping me to achieve a dream.

Brian Ebersole helped me visualize running for political office, and more importantly, he got me seriously involved in politics for the first time in my life. Brian, in semi-retirement mode, travels around Washington State seeking electable candidates. He identified me as a potential candidate one day over lunch, and he kept after me until I at least agreed to see what it was all about. He felt I possessed the attributes needed to run a successful political campaign. If it weren't for him, I doubt I would have ever become involved in the political process.

Another mentor in my life is my dear friend since 2000, **Tim "Good Lookin'" Johnson**, a mentor, role model, friend, and all-around good guy. He calls himself "Good Lookin'" because the name Johnson is so common that he wanted to distinguish himself…especially over the phone when looks don't matter as much. We hold each other accountable; that's what you want in a good friend. We talk almost daily and get together at least once a week when I'm in Tacoma, where he is a prominent businessman.

So as you see, mentors have a way of shaping us and rounding us out to be the best we can be. Mentors add experiences to life and many times spare us from having to go through bad experiences.

You've probably noticed that the majority of mentors in my life have been men, but many women have been mentors to me as well—actually they have probably been in the majority among the great teachers I've had in my life's journey. I think of the wonderful women who introduced me to the world of physical therapy and who, to this day, manage and operate the clinic I own. I think of the outstanding women I work with in various community activities around Seattle and the things we try to accomplish together.

I've always enjoyed the company of people who can teach me a little something I don't already know. I appreciate hanging around people who are a few years older than me, people who have been down the path I'm ready to take, and people who can share insight and experiences to help me along the way.

I encourage you to reach out and find a mentor. Find mentors in your areas of interest and mentors outside your everyday experience. Both will help you to grow and expand your horizons. Also, pay attention to your actions because you never know who might be watching you; it might be someone who could mentor you, or someone who could use a mentor. Someone in your circle of influence (family, neighborhood, or workplace) might admire you, but he or she could be shy about approaching you. Like it or not, you're a role model for others.

Mentoring is a fantastic and rewarding experience. Everybody needs a mentor. Mentor someone who will challenge you, not just a "yes" person who tells you things you want to hear to make you feel better.

I stay very involved with mentoring in the Seattle area. I'm on a statewide mentoring board, the Washington State Mentors (**www.wamentors.org**), and a local mentoring board, the 4C Coalition (**www.the4ccoalition.org**), plus, I mentor a young man at one of the local high schools.

More than ever, children are growing up in homes with negative experiences that can hamper their development and interfere with them fully realizing their potential. Imagine growing up in a home where physical abuse, sexual abuse, emotional abuse, neglect or witnessing domestic violence is prevalent. How about having parents who are mentally ill, depressed, suicidal, drug addicted, alcoholic, incarcerated, or separated/divorced? We don't live in a "Brady Bunch" kind of world anymore. Our children are suffering more than ever, which is why we need to reach out to them and become positive influences in their lives.

Throughout the country, you can find great mentoring organizations in every state. There are several large nationwide mentoring organizations that you can join or support such as Big Brothers/Big Sisters (**www.bbbs.org**) and Boys and Girls Clubs of America (**www.bgca.org**).

Mentoring has been one of the most valuable keys to my success, and as you have seen, my mentors have come from a wide variety of backgrounds. I'm open to listening and learning from all of them, and passing on their wisdom and experience to those I am blessed to mentor.

Chapter 5

EDUCATION & FAITH
SOMEONE IS LOOKING OUT FOR YOU

The difference between school and life? In school, you're taught a lesson and then given a test. In life, you're given a test that teaches you a lesson.
— Tom Bodett

God's promises are like the stars; the darker the night, the brighter they shine.
— David Nicholas

This chapter's message is directed primarily to my younger readers or those who have some influence over them.

I've found two things on my journey through life that will never leave me—my education and my faith. No matter what happens to me, both are always with me. The same may or can be true for you.

As a high achiever all my life, I have found myself surrounded by some people who are attracted to me because of the achievements I've attained—what I've done. They're the type of people who leave you just as quickly when times are bad. I saw that happen when I was with the Dallas Mavericks, at the apex of my career. When I suffered a career-threatening knee injury, all of a sudden, the so-called friends who used to pal around with me just left. They dropped me like a bad habit because it didn't look like I was ever going to play in the NBA again. I quickly learned who my true friends were.

At that time, I also realized that no matter what happened to me personally or in my career, two things would always be with me: what I had learned and what I believe. One is an actual, physical, tangible experience, and the other is part of your personal and spiritual growth. One you can display symbolically on your wall in the form of a diploma, and the other hangs in your inner being. You can take your diploma off the wall and rip it into shreds, but you're still educated. Your faith can be shaken to the core, but when you regain your balance, your faith remains. Education and faith never leave.

Friends come and go. Family members pass away. Fame and fortune can be temporary. Success can be fleeting. Education and faith, if you have them, will be with you throughout your life.

We live in a world where a lot of our inner happiness depends on material things. A designer wardrobe, fancy cars, a big house, and lots of money—that's what we think we need to be happy. But think about it. All those things come and go, or at least, ebb and flow. Are you going to let things you can't always control determine your personal happiness?

In the last few years, our country's economy has shifted seriously. Many people have lost their jobs, their houses, and their cars. Credit ratings have been destroyed; people have become suicidal or suffered from depression. Society is caught up in a crisis no one can control—and many people have attached their personal happiness to the "things" they lost.

When you have an education, you have a document, a diploma, a degree you can show to the rest of the world and say, "Hey, I'm educated and I'm here to compete with the best of them." Even in the midst of life changes—some catastrophic—once things calm down and order is restored, you'll be first in line when opportunities begin to present themselves again, because you have an education.

When I speak to young people, I make sure they understand that an education is vital. It's cool to be educated. Education shows the rest of the world that not only are you smart, but you can hang in there and persevere until you accomplish your goals. Employers love to see that, and everyone else respects that. It's cool to go to school!

If you're an adult, encourage young people to make a promise to themselves that they will at least finish high school and get a diploma. From there, their odds of success are many times greater than if they drop out of high school. Kids who drop out of high school are "least likely to succeed." They're headed for trouble, or as we used to say in church, "up the rough side of the mountain." No one wants to go up the rough side of the mountain. Life is challenging enough as it is. Kids who drop out of school are more likely to get involved with gangs, drugs, teenage pregnancy, early parenthood, unemployment, substance abuse, alcohol, and incarceration. Odds are that their lives (at least lives of quality) will most likely end early. It's not a good way to go. Why fight the odds?

FAITH

I once heard a story that goes something like this:

> Before the beginning of creation, God and Satan had a conversation about the wonderful, marvelous creation of human beings, made in

God's image, that God was about to put into motion. These human beings would love God unconditionally, unfailingly forever.

Satan knew that if God could fully implement His plan, he was doomed. So before God set His plan in motion, Satan said, "God, I ask you to grant me one wish before you create human beings in your image, humans who will love you unconditionally and unfailingly forevermore. If you grant me this one wish, and those humans created by you in your image continue to love you unconditionally forevermore, I will never be a problem for you again."

God thought to Himself, "Now, why would Satan want me to grant him one wish?" God was going to create human beings who were perfect and in His image, and by doing so, there would not be a role or a place for Satan.

So God said, "Satan, what is it you wish for?"

Satan turned to God and said, "Grant me the wish of being able to create doubt in the hearts and minds of these perfect human beings made in your image."

For reasons known only to God and Satan, God granted Satan his one wish.

And that is the only tool Satan has ever used in his battle to win us over and to destroy our faith in God (and in ourselves)—*doubt*.

Doubt weakens your faith. Many things in life create doubt and weaken your faith. Keep in mind that the devil is at work in all of us, eroding the faith we need to **Stand Above the Crowd** and be the best we can be.

Faith is the other element in life that is everlasting. Once you grow to the point where you have some serious faith going on, it will never leave you. Oh sure, there'll be times when your faith will be tested, especially if you put your faith and trust in something or someone who is undeserving of your faith and trust. Let's get this straight right now: There will come a point in your life when people will let you down, no matter what you do to prevent it. *People are people, they've always been that way, and they'll always be that way.* There are just too many variables beyond our control when it comes to dealing with people. So the faith I'm talking about is faith in a Higher Power beyond our comprehension. For a Christian like me, that faith is in God. That doesn't mean that God will always give me my heart's desire when I want it and how I want it. My faith teaches me that God will never let me down, and He has promised never to leave me nor forsake me. That's His promise to all of us.

There will be times when it feels like God has abandoned you. There will be times when you will ask, "Where are you God? Why have you left me?" Mary Stevenson's answer to that question inspired her to write the famous poem "Footprints in the Sand." If you don't know this remarkable and moving poem, please visit **www.footprints-inthe-sand.com.**

There will be times when your faith will be tested. Guaranteed! Life is a journey, and it's going to be filled with difficulties, twists, turns, and obstacles. Besides, Scripture says your life won't exist without trials and tribulations. So you might as well get ready for it.

My Pastor Emeritus, Rev. Samuel B. McKinney, from Mount Zion Baptist Church in Seattle, Washington, is fond of saying, "If you haven't come upon hard times yet, keep on living." That's true, because we don't know what life has to offer us around every twist and turn.

Having strong faith means that no matter what happens, you still have faith that God is in control and that things will work out according to His will. Having faith means humbling yourself and realizing you aren't in control of the majority of things that happen in your life. You don't know when you're going to get a pink slip at the office. You don't know if your health will fail. You don't know if you'll make it safely from home to work and back again. You don't know when a family member will pass on and leave you behind. You don't know how your children will turn out, no matter how you've raised them. You truly don't know who your neighbors are and what they're up to behind closed doors. You can only have faith that the person who shares your marital vows will actually be there "For better, for worse, For richer, for poorer, In sickness and in health, To love and to cherish, 'Till death do us part."

So what do we know for sure in this world? Not anything really.

So we have faith, unshakable, undeniable faith, faith that resonates through and through. You just know things are going to work out. No matter what happens to you, no matter what people do to you, you still know things will be okay. As Rev. McKinney says, "When you know that you know that you know—then you know!" How's that for faith and confidence?

Now, as I pause to take measure of my life, I'm grateful I have had both my education and faith to lean on. Having a college education, however, doesn't mean I stopped learning. On the contrary. For me, going to college was just the beginning of a life of learning. My faith has been tested, along with everyone else's during difficult economic times, but I continue to have faith and try to make the best decisions possible. It's easy to second-guess and have 20-20 hindsight, but I try to stay away from that kind of thinking because it does me no good. What's best for me is to stay focused, keep my faith strong, and lean on God while using the brain and the resources He's given me.

My message to young people is: If you haven't finished your education, it's never too late. Make it a priority. If nothing else, completing your high school or college education gives you a sense of accomplishment and levels the playing field as you go out into the world.

And never stop growing in your faith. Join support groups and participate in fellowship with others who will strengthen and encourage you, especially during challenging times. Learn to recognize what you can and can't control in your life. Instead of asking, "Why me?" when times get tough, take a different look at your situation and say, "God will never give me more than I can bear. He's promised me that."

I heard a great quote, attributed to Winston Churchill, the other day: "A pessimist sees the difficulty in every opportunity; an optimist sees the opportunity in every difficulty." Are you a pessimist or will you be an optimist?

Chapter 6

NUTRITION
EATING RIGHT, FEELING RIGHT, LIVING WELL

It is health that is real wealth and not pieces of gold and silver.
— Tom Bodett

I've been in athletics for more than half of my life. As I described earlier, one of the reasons I started playing basketball at such a late age was because I was probably one of the most unathletic kids you ever want to see growing up.

I was always a big kid. In fact, I came into this world at twenty-four inches and more than eleven pounds (can anybody say *ouch?*). I grew at a steady clip, even though I never went through a significant "growth spurt," so to speak. I always grew two or three inches a year until I was twenty-one years old. I was like most kids, though, because I grew up on a lot of junk food and sugary snacks. Since they were readily available (when budgets are tight that tends to be what fills the cupboards) and quick and easy to prepare, that's what I "feasted" on until we had a family-style meal once or twice a week when we could actually round up everyone into one place.

I'd say my favorite foods growing up were hamburgers, hot dogs, pizza, French fries, cereal by the boxful, potato chips, soda pop, cookies, pies, donuts, and just about anything else that wasn't good for you. Hey, after all, I was a growing boy and I had a lot of body to fill. With my dad being retired from the Air Force most of my growing up years, our family shopped at the commissary on the Air Force base. We had a large, old station wagon, and either my mom or dad would drive with one of us kids out to the base and load that station wagon up from front to back, stacked so high we almost couldn't see out the windows. That's what you have to do to feed a growing, hungry family of four kids, a mom, a dad, and any relatives who drop by.

I grew up "large." People constantly described me as "big-boned," or they would say that I would "grow into" my body and slim down as I got older. On the contrary, I got fatter as I got older until I got involved with athletics in high school.

By the time I reached high school, I was 6'8" and weighed about 330 pounds. No wonder the football coach tried to recruit me to play on the high school football team! I was a good guy, but I wasn't athletic at all, and added to that, I didn't care about athletics. Luckily, Coach Calhoun saw some potential buried deep inside that big frame of mine.

At my athletic peak, when I was about thirty, I weighed 280 pounds with 6 percent body fat, and I was able to run a sub-six-minute mile when I reported for training camp to start the NBA seasons. It was through a lot of hard work and being diligent with my workouts that I was able to attain such peak physical performance.

About that same time, I took up the martial art form of tae kwon do, and I worked at it for about a dozen years, especially during the off-season in preparation for the upcoming NBA grind. When I was with the Dallas Mavericks, one of my black belt tae kwon do friends, Kenn Thorpe, came into the training facility after practice and put me and several other team-mates through tae kwon do workouts. Those workouts were very benefi-cial in helping us to maintain our flexibility and agility, especially as big guys. As I became an older player in the league, I was able to play with more agility instead of brute strength as I had when I was younger. That saved a lot of wear and tear on my body over the years.

I had all the usual dynamics at play, as does anyone who is extra-large in today's society. No matter how I try not to be self-conscious, a sub-conscious voice always reminds me that I don't fit in. I've sat on a chair that couldn't hold my weight, only to have it collapse underneath me. I've passed up booths in restaurants because I realized they'd be too tight to squeeze into. Kids in high school pinched my flesh to see whether I could feel it underneath all the fat I was carrying around. So I know it's tough on any end of the spectrum to try to fit into a society where "one-size-fits-all."

All of us who are outside that "average height, average weight, and aver-age build" parameter have a different reality that reminds us every day that we are who we are and we have to do the best with it that we can. A significant percentage of the U.S. population is obese. Now there is even a "super obese" classification. Those are individuals who weigh more than 500 pounds. I've developed a sensitivity by being able to "feel" what others must go through if they have to deal with challenges such as dis-abilities, extraordinary height/lack of height, extraordinary weight/lack of weight, blindness, and the like. I've been there, and I continue to live a life in which I just "don't quite fit in." I'm reminded of that every time I walk through a standard doorway.

Only when my high school athletic coaches started paying attention to me and pointing out some of my potential did I realize that if I were ever going to tap into that potential, I would have to start losing some weight and figure out how to become the athlete they believed I could be. I started taking an interest in trying to eat a little better and exercising to build muscle. Like every red-blooded American boy, I wanted to have a bunch of muscles that I could flex in the mirror so I would look like my favorite big-time wrestlers, Rocky "Soul Man" Johnson, Ernie Ladd, Hulk Hogan, and a host of others. I started watching the Jack LaLanne exercise shows and even found myself rearranging some furniture so I could do simple things like push-ups and dips to start building the muscular physique I only dreamt of having at the time.

Part of my daily routine was to run several laps around the field that surrounded my high school in Sacramento. I ran four miles a day, cut out all snacks and junk foods, and lost more than a hundred pounds in one year. I continued this routine all through my junior year while getting ready to play basketball for my senior year. That's when the weight really started coming off and I finally started to blossom into the student athlete I would become, an athlete who'd eventually head to the pros. I also started to take daily vitamins and read about the benefits of nutritional supplements.

My interest in nutrition and fitness began in earnest as I got serious about athletics. Every day, I'd be sure to pop my daily vitamins (I soon graduated to a small packet of daily vitamins and supplements) into my mouth and begin my exercise routine, following my favorite Jack LaLanne exercises. As with most things in my life that I get serious about, I made it a lifestyle change, not just the fad of the week. Sure, I tried different diets and exercises, just to mix it up a little. I stayed on that path of trying to attain a better nutritional and fitness level by gathering as much information as possible and implementing it into my life every day.

My basic level and involvement with nutritional supplements was sufficient when I was a youngster and my metabolism allowed me to eat just about anything I wanted, exercise, take supplements, and be good to go. Of course, that's easy to do when you're in your teens and twenties, but my, how things change when you get into your thirties and forties.

I became serious about everything I put into my body when I became a professional athlete. At Washington State University, it was good enough for me to rely on my daily nutritional supplement packet and our excellent team meals. I stayed on top of the latest nutritional information as it came around by studying, attending various seminars, and by asking many questions of the professionals.

My teammates will recall the handfuls of nutritional supplements I took every day during my career. At one point, I was taking more than one hundred different vitamins, amino acids, essential oils, protein tablets and the like every single day! I'd take a handful of thirty-five or so in the morning, another handful during lunch, and another handful in the evening. I had it down to a science. Over the years, as I've learned more about quality vs. quantity and the absorbability factor of supplements (our ability to absorb declines as we age), I've turned to the Isotonix line of nutritional supplements. They have an absorbability rate of 95 percent, instead of the 25-50 percent of most tablets, capsules, and pills. I'm a firm believer in the Isotonix line, and I am certified as a nutritional consultant in the field. Feel free to contact me or click onto my website at **www.marketamerica.com/donaldson** for additional information on the Isotonix line of nutritional supplements.

When I graduated from college and started playing and hanging out with the big boys, I entered a new world of awareness regarding how people take care of themselves. Experts have documented that most athletes can rely solely on their physical ability and continue to have high performance levels until their late twenties, and then they suffer a significant drop-off if they don't take care of themselves. I saw it in the pros. Athletes are notorious for poor eating habits, and we pay the price as we put a demand on our bodies. I've seen world-class athletes have a record-breaking season one year, but the next year, they can barely roll out of bed due to fatigue, injuries, and a lack of energy. It happens quickly and suddenly when you perform at a high level, compared to more subtly for everyday folks. I noticed how poor eating habits affected other athletes, so I was determined to take care of myself to ensure a long career.

One of the first things that athletes reach for as they prepare for competition and training is something to enhance their performance. In recent decades, performance-enhancing supplements have been all the rage in Olympic sports, football, and baseball. You don't hear about them too much in basketball because most basketball players rely on a combination of speed, agility, quickness, and strength. If you lose your flexibility and become muscle-bound, the traits you need for basketball will vanish.

Most basketball athletes find other ways to increase alertness and stamina. Probably the most common "supplement" is caffeine. It's not unusual for guys to drink coffee and soda loaded with caffeine to stay revved up.

When I played in Italy, Spain, and Greece, the most common thing the guys did on the way to the games was to make sure the bus driver stopped at a local café, where we loaded up on espresso drinks before the game. It was a pretty hilarious sight, seeing a group of extremely tall guys standing in line at the counter to get our fill of caffeine. Espresso drinks in Europe are thick and syrupy and put our little wimpy espresso drinks in the United States to shame. Some of my teammates would down several cups by the time we got back on the bus! I remember many a time we were so revved up on caffeine that we were literally shaking at the foul line, trying to shoot free throws. It takes tremendous focus, concentration, and timing to make sure to get off your shot in between shakes!

I never knew anyone personally in the NBA who used performance-enhancing steroids. While I was playing, two or three guys, because of their size, were suspected of using steroids or something along those lines; however, I can confidently say that steroids are not a problem in the NBA.

A few years into my pro career, I became known as a guy who knew about supplementation and basic nutrition. My teammates knew I was interested in taking care of myself with regard to what I was putting in my body. Since I didn't drink, smoke, or use drugs, I was a little bit of an oddball in the NBA, and that was *before* I became a vegetarian! The NBA is a world where as long as you perform, you're welcome to be part of it all.

I've never been much of a coffee drinker, except for an occasional down-ing of a cup or two before games, or with breakfast on Saturday or Sunday. As I studied nutrition and visited specialty shops around the country, I learned about herbal stimulants. I decided to try them. I'm sure quite a few of them are still around in various forms—one of the favorites back then was called Excel, a blend of herbs that was a natu-ral stimulant. I thought it was one of the best all-natural stimulants on the market, and I could actually feel the pick-me-up it gave me during games. Such stimulants, however, are how athletes get themselves into trouble. After all, who takes the time to read labels? Many of us go with what the person in the nutritional store says, or what our trainer gives us. So when the news broke in the 1990s about athletes being involved with performance-enhancing supplements, I knew most of them truly didn't know what they were putting into their bodies, unless it was an illegal substance obtained through a questionable source.

Throughout most of my years in the NBA, I tried natural stimulants from various health food stores. Ginseng was all the rage back in the 1980s, and "power drinks" loaded with caffeine and sugar came next. I appreciated that my teammates put a lot of trust and faith in me; they knew I did my research on these various over-the-counter products. I think at one point, almost everyone on the Dallas Mavericks was on some sort of ginseng product and taking advice from me.

I became a vegetarian shortly after I started to play in Dallas. It began when founder and dear friend Rhonda Holley of the Society of Texas Animal Rights (STAR) asked me to become the organization's spokesperson and the "public face" of its programs. At that point, I didn't know much about animal rights, but I'd been an animal lover all my life. I didn't know anything about animal exploitation other than knowing people were often cruel and irresponsible in how they treated their animals. Issues such as animal rights, factory farming, and animal exploitation were foreign to me.

I agreed to become STAR's spokesperson. My main responsibility was to visit area schools and talk to young people about spaying/neutering programs and responsible pet ownership. Most school-age kids have cats and dogs, so we had a welcoming audience. I learned quickly to keep things tame and didn't go into graphic details. When I attended STAR's monthly meetings, I discovered that almost everyone in the group was either a vegan or a vegetarian. I found it fascinating to listen and learn about a lifestyle I knew nothing about. Imagine being a vegetarian in the heart of Texas—big cattle country!

That's when I decided to become a vegetarian, and I've been a vegetarian for more than twenty-five years now. I tried to talk to my trainer and team doctors about this newfound way of life I was embracing, but they didn't know much about vegetarian diets, other than a rumor that one reason Hall of Famer Bill Walton was plagued with injuries was because he was a vegetarian. I don't think any evidence existed to back that up, but people talked about it anyway. My trainer and the doctors were concerned that if I became a vegetarian, I'd wither away or become injury-prone. At the time, I was one of the biggest and strongest players in the league, so I was concerned about that, too.

As I mentioned earlier, I do my homework when I get serious about attempting to do anything. Becoming a vegetarian was something I was going to be very serious about. I've come across people who say they're vegetarians, but they still eat fish, or they subsist on junk food, which makes them unhealthy. My take is that if you're going to do anything in life, do your homework and do it right. That way, whether it works for you or not, you've had a good, informed opportunity to see for yourself.

I stayed diligent about nutritional supplementation throughout my transition to a vegetarian diet. One key to success is being diligent in everything you do and being sure you have all the tools to be successful. I found nutritional supplements, especially for a very demanding career such as in professional sports, to be essential. I even had my blood analyzed every three or four months to check various amino acid, vitamin, and mineral levels. This stuff fascinates me, and it gives me plenty of information so I can converse with anyone on the subject.

I became a vegetarian over the course of about twelve months. I had already cut back significantly on red meat anyway, so I knew it wouldn't be a big deal to cut back on chicken and fish, too. I learned how to cook terrific vegetarian meals and to order vegetarian dishes at any restaurant in town (even steakhouses) to make sure I stick to my vegetarian diet.

Any fear I had about withering away and not being able to compete at a high level quickly vanished as I noticed an increase in my energy level, and I was able to bounce back from demanding practices and be ready to go again in less than twenty-four hours. I was able to play game after game, and on many occasions, play all forty-eight minutes without feeling fatigued at all. Several competitors asked me whether I was tired during games, as they were bent at the waist trying to catch a breath and I was still standing tall. It was an amazing time, and it was something I was going to be firm about, although I wasn't going to try to shove it down anyone's throat. When the guys asked me why I didn't eat meat, I gave them some basic information about the vegetarian lifestyle/healthy eating and left it at that. I think that I played until I was forty-two is testament to the fact that I was doing something right, and I attribute that to a vegetarian lifestyle.

I think the greatest challenge I had in being a vegetarian was the time I spent playing basketball in Spain. It didn't seem to be much of a challenge in Italy or Greece, where fruit, vegetables, bread, and pasta are the norm. It was different in Spain, especially in certain areas. I lived in Seville one year and Lugo the next, and I can say that during that time I had enough potato omelets and beans to last a lifetime!

As I got into what a vegetarian lifestyle is all about, I learned some of the consequences a meat-based diet has on our environment and our economy, let alone our individual health. If people realized how much food, water, land, and energy go into producing our heavy meat-based diets (at the expense of famine and starvation in other parts of the world), we'd be more apt to make dietary changes. Information is abundant, so I encourage you to research, do your homework, and learn how you can do your part to make our world a better place.

Subscribe to magazines such as *Vegetarian Times* or *E Magazine*, or read books that have pioneered the way such as *Diet for a New America* by John Robbins and *Silent Spring* by Rachel Carson, or take in a movie like *Food Inc.*, and you'll find yourself being amazed by the many things we can do to make our world a better place. It's easier today being a vegetarian/vegan than it was back in the 1970s and 1980s. You still have to use common sense though, eat well-balanced meals, check with your doctor to make sure everything is working well, watch your weight, exercise, and get plenty of rest.

After a recent annual physical, my physician called and left me an extended and enthusiastic voicemail saying he'd never seen blood lipid levels as great as mine, and that whatever I was doing, to keep on doing it. Over the years, I've told him I'm a vegetarian, and that I exercise daily. He told me that it's obviously working for me, and that for a man over fifty years of age, I keep myself in outstanding shape. Of course, like everyone else, I can stand to lose those ten stubborn pounds that don't want to go away, but overall, I'm very happy with the results and the lifestyle that I adopted over twenty-five years ago.

Chapter 7

ACCOUNTABILITY

Accountability. Big word, but what does it mean? It's defined as: "responsibility to someone or for some activity." I'd like to take it a step further and define it as: "responsibility to one's self for every activity one is engaged in."

Growing up, I learned the lessons of accountability early and often. My dad instilled those lessons in me. He, along with my mom, made sure that before I went out, watched my favorite television programs, or ate a bowl of cereal, my chores were done and my homework was up to snuff. On many occasions, the first thing he did when he came home in the evening was check to see whether my chores were done. They were basic childhood chores of cleaning up after the pets, mowing the lawn, picking up my room, and any other chores Mom had lined up for me.

Here are a few lessons I learned, early on, about why it's important to be accountable:

KEYS OFF THE KEY RING

I tell this story often in my speaking engagements, especially with young people who are trying to avoid being accountable. When I was a college freshman at Washington State University, one of the first things Coach Raveling did was to take me into his office. There, he took a couple of keys from his key ring and handed them to me. Back then, anyone with official significance or responsibility carried a key ring that symbolized clout, power, or control; that key ring told you that you needed that person in order to access where you wanted to go. I mean that both literally and figuratively.

Coach Raveling said he was going to give me those keys because he couldn't be with me twenty-four hours a day, seven days a week, nor did he want to be! He told me those two keys would be important along my road to success, and I should, in fact, consider them the keys to my success. Of course, I thought the keys would open up some sort of "magic kingdom" and that I'd be a success overnight. But in actuality, one of the keys opened the weight room. Coach Raveling said I needed to get bigger, stronger, and meaner. I needed to make myself into a better athlete, and the way to do that was to take his keys and hit the weights several hours a day. The other key opened the gymnasium. Coach Raveling told me I needed to get to the gym at least a couple of hours a day, after my homework was done, and after I had eaten dinner. I was to get into the gymnasium and do the basketball drills we'd covered during the week at practice.

I did those drills faithfully for the first couple of years I was at school. People often saw me on campus with a miniature basketball rim, known as a "rebounding ring," and a basketball as I headed to the gymnasium.

That's accountability! It started with following through on my chores and responsibilities without having anyone looking over my shoulder, and making sure I got it done—and it paid off. The same applies to you. Take charge of being accountable. No one will do it for you. It will pay off in the end.

RAISING PETS

One of the best ways for young people to become accountable quickly is to be responsible for the family's pets. I've always been an animal lover and grew up in a household of small pets and animals. We had everything—hamsters and guinea pigs, domestic and trained rats and mice, rabbits and even the occasional chick around Easter time, and of course, plenty of dogs and cats. I was the one who typically took care of the animals. Some of my favorite pets were a flock of homing pigeons that I kept in a pigeon coop in the backyard. At times, I had twenty-five to thirty pigeons and spent countless hours in the backyard with them.

Having pets was a privilege, not a "right" in our house. I learned that the hard way when one day, my mom got fed up with us for not listening to her and not staying on top of our chores. It seemed like no one was really taking care of the animals, so those chores and responsibilities kept falling on her. So she backed up the family station wagon, loaded up several of our cats and dogs, and took them off to the pound. She must've taken three or four dogs and three or four cats to the pound that day. I was heartbroken. A couple of them were my favorite pets, and of course, being a kid, I couldn't understand why my mom was so "mean" at the time. It taught me a harsh lesson, though: If you want to enjoy the pleasures in life, then you have to be responsible and accountable for your behavior at the same time.

GROWING UP CHRISTIAN

I grew up in a very Christian household, and my parents made sure the whole family headed off to Sunday School and church every week. They were the driving force behind making sure we were instilled with the Christian faith and that we grew up in church.

Actually, I enjoyed going to church, and at one point, I taught Sunday School to some of the young people who were a few years younger than me. I've read the Bible cover to cover many times, even as a youngster. My Sunday School teacher saw I was interested in the Bible and was very knowledgeable, so before I knew it, I was teaching Sunday School.

Growing up with a strong faith teaches you to be accountable. You learn to be accountable to God, and you learn that He wants you to be accountable for your actions. If you have a strong belief and faith (no matter what your faith), you tend to do things that (God/your Higher Power) wants you to do. So accountability comes naturally.

HOLDING EACH OTHER ACCOUNTABLE

We never know how we impact those around us when we give them a sense of responsibility and accountability. We all know when we do right and when we do wrong, and I believe that all of us want to be the best we can be. So I urge you to take that step in encouraging everyone around you, including yourself, to be more accountable.

One of the best ways to be accountable to yourself is to surround yourself with people who will hold you accountable. I find that on many occasions, my so-called "celebrity status" precedes me when I become involved in different activities. Many times, people who invite me to join groups and organizations become overly excited because of the little bit of fame and celebrity I've acquired over the years, mainly due to basketball.

I've learned that many people have "self-serving" interests and want to be around you for the wrong reasons if you have something they want. It could be that you're the star athlete at school or the homecoming queen. None of that matters. What does matter is the importance of surrounding yourself with people who offer you a win-win relationship instead of one that serves only their needs, or yours. I've never needed that kind of "fan appreciation," and I appreciate it even less.

Many times, I've literally had to put my hands out and tell people to calm down and realize that just because I have a little celebrity status, I'm no different than they are, and certainly not any better. I tell them that the last thing I need is another fan club of any kind, and that I'd appreciate it if they would hold me accountable to the same standards they hold themselves. My response surprises people, because in our culture and society, we tend to treat "celebrities" differently. We tend to let celebrities almost get away with murder (ahem, I guess on a couple of recent occasions, we actually have—if you know what I mean). Many times, we let people whom we think are important get away with not doing their share of the work in order to make things happen. I've always been the type who relishes rolling up my sleeves and working in the trenches. It's nice that people recognize the work I've done over the years in athletics, business, and the community, but I don't shy away from hard work, and I don't want to be treated any differently.

On your road to success, be accountable and surround yourself with others who will hold you accountable. If others hold you accountable and expect you to do your share of the work, you'll thrive if you are driven to succeed. Your success will be long lasting; long after the novelty of your celebrity, fame, beauty, or superstar skills wear off (and it happens, believe me), you'll be seen on the merits of your hard work and integrity, rather than riding on the coattails of fame. People respect those who work hard and do their share of the work. Some people want to see what they can get out of the situation, and others just feel better being around accomplished people. But for whatever reason, make sure you stay accountable to yourself and have a person or group to whom you can be accountable.

Chapter 8

ATTITUDE

The longer I live, the more I realize the impact of attitude on life.
— Charles Swindoll, pastor, author, educator

In thinking about how to begin this chapter on attitude, one of my favorite quotes by Charles Swindoll came to mind. I like this quote because it really hits home with so many of the things we deal with in everyday life.

I am convinced that life is 10% what happens to me
and 90% how I react to it.
And so it is with you...we are in charge of our attitudes."

Swindoll goes on to say that the one remarkable trait we have a choice about is the attitude we will embrace for that day.

It's true! We get wrapped up in what happens to us instead of focusing on the things we can make happen—with a positive attitude. I get teased quite a bit by a lot of friends who say that I always seem to be up and have a positive outlook on life with my "happy go lucky" approach and a seemingly ever present smile on my face. I'm not overly Pollyannaish by any means, but I learned a long time ago that it takes more muscles in your face to make a frown than it does to make a smile, so why not smile!

I remain optimistic and keep a positive attitude, despite what's going on around me. That doesn't mean that I just sit around and take what life has in store for me; it means doing my part to make life even better. It helps to have a positive and optimistic attitude.

Now, I could get down and dirty with the best of them and point out things that are wrong in life and in society, but I choose not to do that. Again, it's a choice. I think we can all do a better job of maintaining a positive mental attitude toward everything we do in life. We have to remember that how we approach every day, and how we treat each other is a lifestyle choice. The same is true in how we treat our jobs, our neighborhoods, our environment, our health, our bodies, and just about everything that pertains to life…it really is an attitude choice. We must make that choice every day (and just about every hour of the day) until it becomes a positive habit.

Although I have a positive and upbeat attitude, I'm just like everyone else. I can slip back into a negative attitude if I'm not careful. Each of us must make a conscious decision to be positive every waking moment. How do you see the glass? Is it half-full or half-empty? That in itself makes a huge difference! I choose to see the glass half-full.

When I was a freshman at WSU, during one of our games, Coach Raveling asked me whether I wanted to go into the game. As a freshman, I didn't get in a lot of playing time so many times my mind would start wandering while the game would play on. Sometimes, I'd stare at the cheerleaders, and sometimes I'd look around the stands to see whom I could see. I figured, since I wasn't going to play anyway, I might as well occupy myself with a pleasurable distraction. Looking back at it now, I can't believe I even had the nerve to think I deserved to be out there playing at that point in my career, when I was barely good enough to be on the team. Slowly but surely, a negative attitude started to creep up on me.

I was one of those players who usually didn't get to play—unless the game was totally out of hand one way or another. If there were just a few seconds left and we were up or down by fifteen points, that's when the coach would call on me. It was humiliating, and after it happened a few times, I knew I didn't want to be used that way. I wanted to play when it mattered. I didn't want to be thrown in there as a laughingstock.

So here we were at the Far West Basketball Tournament in Portland, Oregon. We were down to the last few seconds and I hadn't played at all. Coach Raveling looked at the bench and asked me, "Would you like to go in?" I remember it vividly. We made eye contact, and I truly believed he was *asking* me, rather than *telling* me to go into the game. I said, "No, I don't want to go into the game," and boy, did he become unglued. I saw him turn and talk to the assistant coaches, muttering something like, "Can you believe that Donaldson? He'll be lucky if he ever plays for us again!"

When we got to the locker room after the game, Coach Raveling was all over me. He was worked up, shouting and yelling at me, saying things like, "When I ask you to go into the game, you'd better answer 'Yes' from now on." His actual words were a little bit more colorful. They don't call it "Locker Room Language" for nothing!

I share that story not just to illustrate for you Coach Raveling's quick temper (I warned you before that he had one), but to let you know that my negative attitude got me into that situation in the first place. We all go through things like that from time to time, but I've learned to be much more conscientious about my attitude at all times and my approach in all situations. It's something we can control if we choose to do so.

Over the years, I've developed more of a can-do attitude. That allows me to keep stretching myself into endeavors sometimes slightly outside my comfort zone. Whether it's deciding to open a new business location, play a musical instrument, or learn a foreign language, it all begins with a positive outlook. I've learned that with the life skills I've accumulated through the years and with a team concept, I can accomplish just about anything I set out to do. Of course, you have to have a positive attitude from the start; otherwise, there's no sense in getting started. It's not fair to you (or the people around you) if you approach a task without a positive attitude because you'll probably stop far short of your potential. It's a shame that far too many of us allow our negative attitudes to take us down over and over again.

I remember hearing a speech several years ago by the Rev. Jesse Jackson in which he mentioned that "If we do our best, then God will do the rest...anything less than our best is a sin." We can only do our best by having a positive attitude and believing that we can do all things with God's help.

So, you need to have a game plan of sorts—the proper attitude and a great team of people to cheer you on and ensure you'll be successful in anything you take on in life. I've made sure I had both in everything I've done over the years. Whether it is sports, politics, community involvement, or business, a can-do and positive attitude will get you much farther than anything else you can imagine.

In a favorite essay of mine by Charles Swindoll, one of the most poignant lines to me is, "We cannot change our past." Our past is a part of us—no matter whether we like it or not, and no matter where we go in life.

When I was in my early thirties, I undertook the task of trying to discover who I was as a person, as well as whom I was ethnically and culturally. The more I learned about my ancestors' trials and tribulations, many of whom took that horrific journey from Africa to the Americas during the slave trade era, the angrier I became—not only at what had happened during that pivotal time, but also at what persists to this day. I began to understand, with more of a global perspective, that African-Americans in the United States have had to overcome terrific challenges to experience an equal playing field.

At one point in my life, I was an angry young black man, trying to navigate my way through parts of society that could easily have become a minefield of self-destruction or sabotage due to the frustrations I could have encountered had I not been careful. Our prison system is overflowing with people who got tangled up in that self-destructive minefield by letting themselves have the wrong attitude around the frustrations that run rampant in and out of their lives. As I studied more about the history of African-Americans in the United States and the legacy of slavery that somewhat still persists today, I saw in many ways how our society could be unjust when it comes to people of color and to people who are considered the "have-nots."

Mind you, I was never an outwardly rebellious type or the type to complain, "The man is keeping me down." However, I remember reading any book I could get my hands on pertaining to the struggles and plight of African-Americans. I read books about black leaders throughout

American history, including Martin Luther King Jr. and his wife Coretta Scott King, Malcolm X., Shirley Chisholm, Louis Farrakhan, Sojourner Truth, W.E.B. DuBois, and Frederick Douglass, just to name a few. I wanted to put into context what was causing my frustration.

My parents, in trying to shield my siblings and me from life's harsh realities and spare us some of the pain they had endured, did not share much of what it was like for them growing up. I didn't necessarily grow up angry and frustrated with the "system," but it didn't take long for me to run smack into racism and racist attitudes, especially once I left Sacramento for school in Pullman, Washington and the Pacific Northwest, where diversity was and still is in short supply in many instances.

After several years of frustration in dealing with "the system," I realized I didn't want to be the victim. Instead, I decided to be "the victor" in my life's journey. As I surrounded myself with more knowledgeable and positive influences, I began to smooth out some of my rough edges and deal with the anger and frustration pent up inside me. Instead of letting frustration tear me up, I channeled that negative energy into positive energy. I channeled that negative energy into the game of basketball and sports. I turned things around, from potentially self-destructive, to *constructive*, behaviors.

The best way I found to deal with my struggles and frustrations was to change my attitude. When I say I changed my attitude, I don't mean I changed who I am; I changed the way I view the world and the way the world views me. It also means I worked to educate and inform myself so I had a broad perspective and depth of knowledge. Young people, please note: Whatever problems you face in life, you can make them easier and overcome them if you adjust your attitude, educate yourself, and look at things from a broader perspective, not just seeing the problem or situation at hand, but the bigger picture.

I find it's easier to navigate through societal issues of every type if I aim for a broader and deeper outlook on things. I am a member on many boards and committees where I'm the only person of color. Instead of letting it bother me, I welcome the challenge of bridging the divide and welcoming other people of color (and other walks of life) onto the boards and committees. Sure, it's frustrating at times; many times there's no one else in the room to talk with (or at least relate to on a deeper, societal level)—no one who innately understands the challenges and frustrations of trying to change the status quo—but I am there trying to make it easier for others who will come after me.

I make friends easily, so I always seem to find people who are compassionate and want to help make a difference. That's good, and if we have a moment to talk about it (usually brought about by the other person's curiosity), we often find ourselves in deep and enlightening conversation. Here is where having a positive attitude comes in handy because it gives you the ability to work with every situation and with people from all walks of life, whether they are like you or totally different from you.

I'm still socially conscious and aware of the injustices done, not only in the United States, but throughout the world, to talented individuals who aren't given an equal opportunity to compete, compared to those who are given an opportunity simply because they are born into privilege. So, my goal is to make a difference on every board and every committee where I serve.

The following line from Martin Luther King Jr.'s "I Have a Dream" speech exemplifies what this world can look like if we keep working toward it.

"I have a dream that my four children will one day live in a nation where they will not be judged by the color of their skin but by the content of their character."

It's not good enough for me to be a "token" in an organization so they can say, "We've done our part as far as diversity is concerned." What I want to do at every opportunity I get is not only to open the doors to boardrooms and committees, but to create a welcoming environment so people on the outside will feel more comfortable about coming inside.

It's not enough to have the doors open so the outside can peer in, yet not participate. Talk about frustration! One of the most annoying things I've observed is when people of color finally make it into a boardroom or committee room, only to turn a seemingly blind eye and not put a hand out to help another person who may not be represented around the table. It's as if they forget where they came from and the continued challenges of people around them. That's frustration!

We can all do a better job of inclusion and helping to diversify our communities and society if we remember those who don't have an equal opportunity or the access we might have. Remember, don't offer a "handout"; instead, offer a "hand up" so the person you're helping can have fish—not just for today—but more importantly can be taught to fish so he or she will have fish for a lifetime.

With a good attitude, you can overcome just about any obstacle put in front of you. So my message to young people, and even more specifically to young people of color, is this: Remember that the one thing you can absolutely control…is your attitude.

Let me give it to you straight here. Face it, you won't be able to control your parents, your teachers, your coaches, and most people who are a little bit older than you are. Do we have that straight? Sure, you can try all you want to control those elements in your life. But the truth is that I've seen few, if any, examples of young people (up to the age of eighteen) who took control of their parents, teachers, and coaches and have turned that into a positive environment for growth.

You'll need a certain element of trust in others and yourself at this critical phase of your life to prevent yourself from taking a long detour in order to find success. The vast majority of the adults in your life are rooting for you, so it's never too late as long as you maintain a positive attitude. Why take the risk to get off track and then hope to get back on track later—and after how many babies? How much jail time? How much frustration of not finding a job because you didn't finish school? Why take that route? Developing a positive and proper attitude will go a long way toward making this passage from childhood to young adulthood much easier.

I have to take my hat off to young people; they have the benefit of being able to mess up numerous times and still get back on track, simply because they're young. Keep in mind, though, that that scenario only works until you begin to have dependents who need you. So before you even go there, think about how your life will change overnight and how your independence will be hampered if you have a child as a teenager? While you're at it, think about what would happen if you ran away from home and weren't welcomed back? Or, what would happen if you became involved with gangs and the criminal element, such as drugs, prostitution, and pimping?

I know what you're thinking. What you're thinking is, "That won't happen to me because that stuff happens to other kids, and they're dumb." Let me tell you, you'll be lucky—*nothing more*—if you get involved in this stuff and come out in one piece. Remember, I used to be young myself, so I happen to know what I'm talking about.

Let me illustrate for you the power that making one mistake can have. I'm an honorary Commander at McChord Air Force Base in Tacoma, Washington. One day, I had the chance to go out on an Air Force C-17 cargo plane. Now these are the serious workhorses of the United States Air Force. They carry cargo, our troops, tanks, and supplies all around the world. They're built to last, and these planes are heavy duty! It feels like you're inside a tank that's able to fly through the air at 600 miles per hour.

One of the most exhilarating experiences I've ever had was when we returned from a flight across Washington State back to McChord. In order to land, we had to bank sharply in a tight amount of air space, circle until we were close to the ground, and then the pilot skillfully had to level us out at a couple of thousand feet, and land that baby right on the landing strip. I'm using this experience to show you what it's like to be in a serious downward spiral. Granted, the pilot had a lot of skill and previous experience at pulling out of a downward spiral to land on the tarmac. It would have been a disaster if he had made even one mistake. Not only for us on the plane, but for everyone below on the ground.

You don't want to get caught up in a downward spiral unless you have absolute control of the situation. Getting involved with things such as drugs, gangs, dropping out of school, early and unplanned pregnancies, incarceration in our juvenile detention or prison system, and anything else that leads to falling off that pathway to success (no matter how temporary you think it might be) is something you don't want to do. I've told you how I was called every name in the book because I wouldn't "go along to get along" with a lot of my childhood friends and peers. Remember, unless people have your best interests at heart, be cautious and wary of what they want you to do, or what they want from you.

Our attitudes control our lives. Attitudes are a secret power within us. It is of paramount importance that we know how to harness and control this great force, and we do so by developing an attitude that is positive and encourages us to believe in ourselves.

A great way to begin developing your positive attitude is to go online and google Charles Swindoll's "Attitude." Print it out so you have it handy. Post it on your bedroom wall and in your office cubicle. Put it in a place where you can see it and read it every day of the week. Try to memorize a little segment of it every day. Remind yourself that even though you might not have the best education, all the money you'd like to have, the success you dream about, or the perfect circumstances—right now—the one thing you do have, and the one thing you can control, is your attitude. It'll be with you for a lifetime, and it can be one of your best friends!

Chapter 9

NEVER BE SATISFIED

In 1979, I was a senior at Washington State University and we were on our way to Los Angeles to play a weekend set of games against UCLA and USC. As a senior, and the only senior on the team at that time, I was coming into my own as a college athlete. It had been a long road from my beginnings at Luther Burbank High School to essentially sitting on the bench at Washington State University during my freshman and sophomore years. But as a junior and senior, I finally felt good about my abilities as a player, and I was finally able to tap into some of that potential my coaches had seen in me all along.

I was never cocky, arrogant, or self-indulgent, but I'd started to feel a certain confidence about my abilities, as they were starting to blossom at a rapid pace. In my junior year, I had become one of the all-time leading rebounders and shot blockers in Washington State University history. As a senior, I was poised and ready to do even more.

Washington State University had some very good teams during the years I was there (1975 to 1979). Although historically never a basketball powerhouse, our teams were finally able to compete against some of the great teams in the Pacific-10 Conference. UCLA, a basketball dynasty in the '60s and '70s, was the perennial powerhouse. Several other teams in the conference, such as USC, Oregon State, Oregon, University of Washington, and two relatively new Pac-10 members, Arizona and Arizona State, all seemed to be vying for second, third, and fourth place during the years I played at Washington State University. The NCAA Basketball Tournament still accepted only the conference winner and runner-up, plus a handful of independents, for a total of thirty-two teams. Consequently, a lot of good teams never got to experience what it was like to play in the NCAA Tournament, and unfortunately, Washington State University was one of them. It wasn't until several years later that the NCAA Tournament opened up to sixty-four teams.

As we went down to Los Angeles to play our weekend set of games against UCLA and USC, we were actually favored to come back with a couple of victories. Coach Raveling did his best to prepare us to return with victory in hand. I was at the top of my game and was a vital part of our team's success with my rebounding, shot-blocking, and defending.

We got down to Los Angeles and opened up our weekend series against USC. I guess the bottom fell out from there. Not only did I play possibly the worst game ever, but I also handed a career night to the opponent I played against. When we say "giving an opponent a career night," it means he turned in a performance that no one would've thought him capable of. The most embarrassing aspect of not effectively defending someone is when you let him make a career night out of you.

We were favored to win that game, only to get blown out by about twenty-five points! We were in shock, but we managed to shake it off in order to prepare for the game the next night. One thing athletics does is help you develop the ability to bounce back from adversity rather quickly, especially when you have back-to-back games in hostile territory.

The next night against UCLA, we didn't fare much better. I again turned in one of the most horrific performances of my career. I went from my usual average of twelve to fifteen points and ten to twelve rebounds, plus a couple of block shots, to pathetic performances in both games—about six points and four rebounds, and foul trouble throughout. Again, I gave the guy I was playing against a career night. Again we lost by twenty-five points to a team we were favored to defeat.

By then, all of us were down in the dumps and didn't quite understand what had happened. There was nothing we could do except lick our wounds and prepare for the long flight back to Pullman, Washington.

I took it especially hard because I just couldn't understand why we'd lost so badly, or why I had played so poorly. I found myself shortly after the game in the hallway, leaning up against the wall as I waited for my teammates to finish showering and gather on the bus. After a hard defeat, many players find themselves lingering in the shower in an almost ritualistic way of washing that bad karma away and down the drain, but I stuck to my usual routine of getting in and out of the shower quickly and making my way to the bus.

Assistant Coach Pugliese caught me in the hallway and wanted to have a few words with me. I could tell from the look in his eyes that he was serious. I was perplexed, not really knowing what to do or what to say. I just wanted the rest of the guys to board the bus so we could get the heck out of there. I realized I'd played poorly and that we had gotten beaten to smithereens by two teams we were favored to defeat, even on their home courts. Then Coach Pugliese came up alongside me, all 5'7" of him, looked me in the eyes, and asked, "Do you know what happened out there? Do you know why?"

It was no time for me to be a smart-aleck. I knew what he meant, although I waited for him to ask me again. Then I actually started to tear up a bit as I feebly responded, "No, Coach, I don't know what happened out there or why I played so poorly." I was at a loss for words as he saw I was bothered and hurting by the performances I had turned in.

Coach Pugliese, still staring into my eyes, told me I had played that way because I'd become "satisfied." He told me flat out, "James, you became satisfied. You became satisfied with where you are at this stage in your development as a student athlete. What you don't realize is that you have a long way to go if you're going to be successful at this game and in life. You became satisfied!" He held out his hands, and in a very stereotypical Italian fashion, gestured wildly, demonstrating where I was (holding one hand about waist-high) and where I needed to be (holding his other hand over his head).

That night, Coach Pugliese gave me the "Come to Jesus" talk I needed at that crucial phase of my athletic career. The last thing he wanted me to do was brush my poor performance under the rug and act as if it had never happened, like so many of my teammates had done throughout their careers. Pugliese saw I was a good guy with a tremendous upside. He didn't want to see that pissed away because I didn't take it seriously, or because I had become satisfied.

To this day, I've never forgotten that lesson. I've carried it throughout my life into every endeavor I approach. In the back of my head and in all my endeavors, Coach Pugliese's words constantly resonate, "Never be satisfied!"

Chapter 10

FIGHTING FOR WHAT YOU WANT IN LIFE

(THEY CALL ME "DUKES")

As a young person, I was constantly being reprimanded for getting into fights in school and on the playground. In fact, I can take you all the way back to my early days in first grade when I was pulled aside by the teacher and spoken to by the principal, who told me I shouldn't beat up on the other kids anymore because I was much bigger than they were. Now, teachers and principals don't usually see the provoking that leads up to the escalation of fisticuffs, but that's par for the course. I do remember on many occasions being provoked by other kids at school, mainly because I was the biggest kid in the school!

So I grew up with the mindset that because of my size, I really shouldn't be picking on and punching any of the other kids. The impact that understanding had on me was partially to make me isolate myself from the other kids; I grew up to be a very shy and introverted person, and I was often a loner who preferred isolation to social contact. Like most young people, I was learning how to maneuver and navigate the delicate path I had to take through life where teasing from other kids could not mean retaliating by beating the living daylights out of them. In short, I had to learn to control my temper and my attitude, as well as learn how to use my large size to my benefit—beating up other kids might have seemed beneficial when they teased me, but after the principal talked to me, I realized it would only hurt me in the long run.

When I finally got involved in sports, I learned how to use my size to my advantage. At first, while I had this huge physical presence, I didn't feel very comfortable in my body. My coaches saw tremendous potential within me, but inside I was just a timid little boy. Were it not for my physical size advantage, which made my coaches take notice, I might never have discovered all the talents and potential inside of me, much less have had a professional basketball career.

As a college athlete at Washington State University, I finally started coming into my own and feeling pretty comfortable with my size and strength. One of those keys Coach Raveling gave me off of his key ring started paying dividends by the time I was a sophomore in college. When I got to WSU, I stood 6'11" and weighed in at about 220 pounds. By the time I graduated, I was 7'2" and weighed in at 285. That was from those weights that were thrown around in the weight room, not with the wimpy basketball guys, but with the big boys on the football team. Matter-of-fact, I got to the point where I joined the exclusive 300/600 club. You're allowed entry into that club only if you're able to bench press at least 300 pounds and squat at least 600 pounds. I was a proud SOB to be able to do that!

I started really having to stand up for myself and fight when I became an accomplished student athlete and started feeling some of the potential that my coaches had seen in me way before I did.

One of my favorite coaches at Washington State University was one of our assistant coaches, Mark Edwards. He was the young coach on the coaching staff and the one with whom the players felt most comfortable.

We had a lot of fun with him. Coach Edwards would encourage me to get out there and just flail away my elbows, get mean and tough, and take possession of the ball. I wasn't as coordinated at the time, so on many occasions my elbow made contact with someone's head, eye, or nose. Since I had sharp elbows, sometimes I would even draw some blood. Coach Edwards actually kept a running list (it ended up being well over a dozen) of all the guys I had inadvertently (and on a few occasions purposely) injured with a sharp elbow. It got to be pretty humorous at times (especially with Coach Edward's sense of humor), but at the same time, he encouraged me to keep on going and "don't take no stuff on the basketball court." After a while, I grew to embrace that attitude and I have pledged to myself never to back down again.

I remember playing very hard and physical against our starting center at the time, Steve Puidokas. Big Steve didn't like that kind of stuff, especially from an up and coming guy like me. But I didn't let that stop me. I was quickly growing into my own and started to feel very comfortable with my physical size, height, and strength. With my coaches' help, the potential I'd had all along was finally starting to show.

I didn't actually start "fighting" per se until I got to the NBA; then I had to fight and scrape every step of the way. In college, it was almost good enough to be bigger, stronger, and tougher than most of the guys, especially since I was playing against players who were typically a little bit smaller than me. Plus in college, the rules are a lot tighter and the game is called a lot closer, so it's very rare for a physical confrontation to get out of hand. But not in the NBA!

My teammate, Greg Kelser, gave me my nickname "Dukes." Greg and I were young upstarts playing with the Seattle SuperSonics. We both had to do a lot of scraping and clawing to hang in there with the big boys. Greg was actually a first-round draft pick from Michigan State (he was Magic Johnson's former teammate and very good friend), so he had it a little bit easier than I did, but he also played the small forward position in which he went against guys like John "J.J." Johnson, Wally Walker, Danny Vranes, and the like. I had to go against guys like Jack Sikma, Dennis Awtrey, and perhaps the one player I really feared, Lonnie Shelton. Shelton had such a mean streak in him that you never knew when he was in a good mood or not, and everyone was afraid to test him to find out. I had to match up against him quite a bit of the time because we couldn't afford to have him wearing out the starters who were needed to play in the upcoming games, so being a rookie, I drew the unlucky assignment more times than I care to remember.

So life is a little bit different for "the bigs" (the pivot man and the 5-position) than it is for every other position out there in the court. Big guys, just by the nature of the game, have to play much more physically than any other players on the court. We're fighting for position, defending the area around the basket, picking up players as they drive around the perimeter defenders to the basket, as well as trying to muscle our opponent away from the basket and outside the three-second area. We have to wear a multitude of hats, and a lot of our work in the trenches goes unnoticed. True big guys learn not to whine about it. We just roll up our sleeves, put our hard hats on, and go to work. I was tailor-made for that!

I quickly got a reputation for not backing down from anyone as I was finding my way around the NBA as a rookie and second-year man. My very first game as an NBA rookie was against Kareem Abdul-Jabbar, the legendary center and all-time NBA scoring leader for the Los Angeles Lakers. Sure I was nervous, with my knees shaking and my palms all sweaty as I lined up against him on the foul line to try to box him out. Luckily, Kareem wasn't the most physical center in the league or he would have destroyed and dominated me even more so than he did with his pure grace and athletic ability.

Some centers in the league played a very physical game. I recall one game my rookie year, several weeks after encountering Kareem, when we played against the Washington Bullets and their twin tandem of big guys, Elvin "Big E" Hayes and Wes Unseld. Now those were a couple of guys who were out to hurt me; I recall them whispering to each other just outside of my peripheral vision about what they were going to do. Seconds later, as I was going up for a rebound, one of them hit me high and the other one hit below, leveling me out about six feet up in the air. Bam! Down I came on the hardwood in a heap, stunned and bruised, with my breath knocked out of me. That was my first lesson in the NBA that it was a big boys game, and your opponents weren't there to help you be better or to show them up—they were there to try to hurt you so you would go down.

From that point on, as I picked myself up from the ground without an ounce of assistance from Hayes or Unseld, I realized none of my team-mates were going to spring off the bench to come to my defense. I would have to defend myself if I were going to make it in this league, so I decided then never to back down.

I got into several fisticuffs my first couple of years in the league as I was constantly getting tangled up with other big guys while we were wrestling for the ball, going for rebounds, or just fighting for position.

Then came the game, during my second year with the Seattle SuperSonics, when I truly earned my nickname "Dukes." We were playing against the

San Diego Clippers, and I was matched up against very talented, but sometimes temperamental, Tom Chambers. Now Tom and I had very different kinds of games, so I'm sure we frustrated each other to no end in even pretending to guard each other. Tom, at 6'11", could run the floor with the speed and grace of a gazelle, and jump out of the gym. He also could put the ball on the floor and shoot from inside and outside. So he was a handful for anyone to try to slow down. My best hope of slowing him down was to "lay some lumber" (in other words, be physical with him and make sure my body stayed in contact with his as often as possible so I could wear him down before he could beat me). Tom, being somewhat hotheaded, quickly got frustrated with that, especially when the refs didn't heed his whining and complaining.

At one point in the game when we both went up for a rebound, Tom snuck in a cheap shot at me while we were both in midair, but by the time we had landed, I had tagged him good. He didn't like that, but he couldn't do much about it since I was so much bigger and stronger than him. But he did start coming after me, as did several of his teammates. I was backpedaling into one of the corners of the court, just staying out of harm's way while lashing out with some left jabs and tagging everyone who was within reach. We ended up going off the court and into the first row or two of seats at courtside before the referees could even begin to slow things down. I didn't have time to look around for my teammates, and that was a good thing, because none of them were coming to my assistance. It was me against Tom and three or four of his teammates (Joe "Jelly Bean" Bryant, Al Wood, etc.). After everything had calmed down in what seemed like an eternity of fists flying (but as is customary in the NBA, rarely connecting) and bodies charging, I emerged from the whole thing without anyone ever laying a hand on me. That really infuriated

Tom Chambers! From that day on, Greg Kelser and the rest of my team-mates, and virtually all my teammates on the teams I would play on in the future, called me "Dukes."

I realized then that when you work so hard for something for so long, and it means that much to you, you've got to fight for what you want. You've got to fight to hang in there and stay on top of your game. You've got to fight so your competitors won't take it away from you. You've got to fight so your teammates will respect the fact that you're willing to sacrifice for your team. You've got to fight so you don't get "punked" out there on the field/court/diamond or whatever venue you might find yourself playing on.

As my career continued, I was able to establish one of the longest all-time consecutive playing streaks. I ended my career in the top ten players with over 600 consecutive games played. That was a mark of pride for me because I accomplished it by playing through aches and pains, stresses and strains, personal issues from time to time, good teams and bad teams, and everything imaginable in between. I fought for that streak long and hard. One of the things that drives me batty is when either coaches or players elect not to have players play during the last couple of games of the season so they can "save themselves" for the playoffs. Ridiculous! I played through thick and thin no matter what.

But guess what? That streak that I took so much pride in came to a crashing halt because of a fight I got into with Mark West of the Phoenix Suns during a game. Even so, I'd rather have my streak come to an end because of a fight than because I wanted to "save myself" for anything. I've always had the mindset that you have to give it all you've got to give today, and you worry about tomorrow when tomorrow gets here.

I have calmed down quite a bit since my rough and tumble days on the court. As a matter of fact, I recently attended a reunion of retired NBA players (The Legends of Basketball, aka: NBA Retired Players Association) and several of the guys (James Worthy, Magic Johnson, Danny Schayes, Steve Hayes, Joe Barry Carroll, Tom Hammond, and Mark Eaton) all made comments about how they still have bumps and bruises from playing against me. It brought back a lot of memories, and I told some of them that I actually enjoyed hitting them upside the head on the court, but off the court, I'm a nice guy.

I never played with a sense of anger, though, so I always felt under control. In fact, basketball was a great release for me when dealing with life's frustrations. That feeling of release is part of the reason why I still work out every day.

At times, I would even use off court frustrations to motivate me in my game. The frustrations might have been with a coach with whom I didn't get along, or a girlfriend who was frustrating me. In any case, life's frustrations can be a great motivator if you channel that frustration into the proper direction.

I have learned to channel life's frustrations into a motivating force for me in everything I try to accomplish. I learned a long time ago not to back down and to "go for it." What's the worst thing that can happen? What, I might lose? Guess what? I just might win also!

At times, you really have to step up and fight for what you want in life. Fighting doesn't mean it has to resort to fisticuffs or verbal sparring, but you will have to take a stand. Are you willing to fight for what you want in life? Are you willing to do it? You're capable and able, but are you willing? Successful people are usually on the offensive and are willing to fight for what they want in life; they are the people you'll end up competing against when it comes down to it.

There's no need to fight dirty (and I don't encourage it anyway), but you'll find yourself pushing yourself further than you ever imagined if you resolve never to back down.

Stand up for what you want in life and you'll end up a winner!

Chapter 11

IF YOU WANT TO PLAY IN THE PROS

Anyone can give up; it's the easiest thing in the world to do.
But to hold it together when everyone else would understand if you fell
apart, that's true strength.
— Author Unknown

Sports do not build character. They reveal it.
— John Wooden

Most people take one look at me and figure I was born to be a pro, but that's so far from the truth. If they knew my story, they'd know that becoming a pro was the furthest thing from my mind, and certainly not a sure bet, even after I finally decided to play basketball.

I was fortunate enough to grow up in a stable family. That gave me a great start. Plus, being blessed with extraordinary height, but not necessarily the athletic ability to go with it; fortunately, I had help from others who pointed me in that direction. Most of the time, they did so for their own personal agendas, not because playing basketball was necessarily what I wanted. I didn't even have a strong desire to play organized ball until my last year in high school. So, at least for me, I was late to the game and any "pro" aspirations.

Today, I enjoy speaking to young athletes. It's exciting to see them dream about becoming pros one day. I hope all of them realize their dreams—if that's what they truly want. Some say it's easier to become a brain surgeon than to become a professional athlete. But that doesn't stop people (nor should it) from dreaming and imagining that they have what it takes.

It does take a lot of dedication to become a professional athlete, and since I've been there, I'd like to shed some light here on what it is really like to be a pro.

GETTING TO THE NEXT LEVEL

Most young athletes fail to realize that as they dream about becoming pros, tens of thousands of young people in America have the same goal. That is just a fact; I don't say it to dissuade anyone from pursuing his or her dream.

If you dream of becoming a professional athlete, I want you to realize that as you move to the next level, from middle school, to high school, to the college/university level, and then finally on to the pros, your work becomes more challenging and your competition greater. You'll have to be able to respond to the challenges and improve your game along the way. I often see young athletes who, because they dominate at one level, then automatically assume they will dominate at the next without making any improvements. Seek out the best competition so you can prove yourself at every level. There will always be someone better than you, and if there's not at the moment, there soon will be, so improving your skills and game is an ongoing process.

As you move up the ranks, you'll see the natural ascension that takes place. Good athletes, and those with raw physical skills, can simply get by in middle school and high school. You first really notice the separation when it's time for an athlete to try to move on from high school to college. The competition really sets in when the recruiting wars begin for those college scholarships.

Professional recruiters naturally look at athletes from the *major* colleges and universities, but that's not always the case. Athletes at smaller schools get noticed too. Dozens of athletes come from smaller colleges who get a chance to move to the pros because they possess that "something special" and the recruiters notice it. So no matter what your level, **Stand Above the Crowd** and take advantage of every opportunity you're given to highlight your skills because you never know who might be watching and evaluating you.

Another thing that separates those who do move on to the pros from those who don't is *who wants it most.* Unless you're a first- or second-round draft pick, you will have to work your tail off to prove your worth. There will be times when you will be tested and there will be times when you'll feel like you're not being treated fairly, but you have to rise above that. I can't begin to tell you how many times I saw guys arrive at training camp thinking they could ride in on their high school and college accomplishments. You can pick them out of the crowd easily; they're the ones who have that "cool" strut. When you get these guys in a conversation, nine times out of ten, they talk about their glory days instead of the job at hand.

You'll have to put your past behind you. Instead, focus on why you're there. You're about to run into a buzz saw of competition. You're going to face athletes with families to feed, mortgages to pay, and—come hell or high water—they're not going to surrender their positions to *you.* You're also going to go up against athletes whose lifelong dream, just like yours, is to make it to the pros. I'll mention time and again the importance of never being satisfied. You'll find that many athletes become satisfied as soon as they earn a spot on the team and the paychecks start rolling in. Being satisfied is usually when they become vulnerable—and when you can go at them with a vengeance.

YOU'LL BE TESTED ALONG THE WAY

I already told you about how during my rookie year I had to go up against Kareem Abdul-Jabbar, and also how Elvin Hayes and Wes Unseld from the Washington Bullets sent me crashing to the floor. Those were moments early in my career when I was tested to see what I would do next. I had the choice either to tuck in my tail and run, or to pick myself up, dust myself off, and keep going. Obviously, I chose the latter, and by doing so, I came to understand that to prove myself and to gain the respect of my competitors, I had to hang in there no matter what.

I had classic battles against the "Bad Boys" from the Detroit Pistons on many occasions. Bill "McFilthy" Laimbeer and Rick "McNasty" Mahorn were the baddest of the Bad Boys. When you played against those two, you were in for a long night. I truly believe those two really enjoyed mixing it up and daring you to hit them "upside the head." If you did, they'd just shrug it off and give you one of those "Is that all you got?" smiles.

On one occasion, Laimbeer and I got tangled up going for a rebound; neither of us was going to give in and let the other have the ball. We wrestled until one of the referees stepped in to try to pry us apart. At just that instant, our momentum carried us into the referee and we blew his knee out. I can only imagine what it must have felt like for that referee as two seven-footers (and a combined total of nearly 600 pounds) crashed down on top of him. He lay in pain, clasping his knee while Bill and I still wrestled on the hardwood and just wouldn't let go of the ball (or each other).

My career was full of moments like that, where I had to prove myself. Your career will also be full of moments where you'll have to prove yourself. You always have the option and the choice of hanging in there or packing it up and calling it a day. I earned the nickname "Dukes" because I was never one to back down from anyone, and I hung in there, no matter what. Sure, some guys intimidated me and I was afraid to play against them, but I wouldn't let them know that, so I kept on competing.

MAKING SACRIFICES IS PART OF THE GAME

If you dedicate yourself to becoming the best you can be, you'll find that you'll have to make tremendous sacrifices along the way. I grew up in a time when sacrifices were expected of the players. That's not so much the case anymore, and coaches don't dare to "ride" players the way they used to. But that's all the more reason why it's important for the athlete to learn to sacrifice immediate gratification for greater rewards in the future—it will keep you a step ahead of the competition.

In college, my friends left me behind just about every weekend as they went to parties around campus. I stayed behind to work on my game— lifting weights, studying my playbook, watching game films, or just getting some rest. Sure, I felt I was missing things, but I didn't dare let anything take me off my road to being successful and achieving my goals. I know it's tough to discipline yourself, but that's what it takes to be a pro. The parties and the beautiful people you feel you're missing now will be there in abundance once you become a successful pro. So keep that in mind, and realize that those things you're sacrificing now will reappear for you in the end.

When you're a success, everyone wants to be around you. When you're a bust, then you'll find out the hard and humiliating way just who your true friends are. I say be a success and carefully select who you want to surround yourself with. You'll have the best of both worlds!

DON'T LET SUCCESS GO TO YOUR HEAD

Finally, once you make it, don't let success go to your head. As I've said before, someone is always there waiting to pull you down, and that doesn't just mean during the game. People want to use you for their own ends; they want to be your friend only because you're famous and successful, and they want to see what they can get out of you. Use common sense in everything you do, both on the court and off it. I'm going to close this chapter with the following list of rules my good friend Greg Guedel wrote to help professional athletes stay on top: before, during, and after their professional careers.

10 RULES FOR THE ELITE ATHLETE

By Greg Guedel

Professional sports is a collection of multi-billion dollar industries, and the search for new talent gets more intense and competitive every year. It's not uncommon for scouts to begin watching promising athletes as early as middle school, and if you have elite talent, you'll soon find yourself with an ever-growing circle of "friends." A few of these people may be genuinely interested in helping you develop and achieve your potential, but most are simply out to get money—*your* money.

The word "Pro" is short for professional. You need to approach your athletic career as a professional enterprise. The moment you receive your first paycheck, you have created a business: "You, Incorporated." Just like any other business, you must manage it intelligently in order for it to grow and prosper. The following ten rules are collected from my experiences and the advice of my legal and business partners. Following these rules will help you to steer clear of the problems that derail careers, and give you fundamental principles for managing your success.

1. Never sign anything you don't understand. If the terms of a contract or other legal document aren't clear, keep asking questions until you understand everything completely. Some people feel shy or silly about asking questions, or they are afraid they won't look smart if they do. I guarantee you'll feel a lot worse if you sign a bad contract, so forget that kind of thinking and be sure before you sign.

2. Always read every contract before you sign it. Never mind somebody who says, "This is our standard agreement" or "Don't worry; everybody signs this same deal." Just because somebody else signed the deal doesn't mean it's a good deal for you. Make sure the agreement is consistent with your goals and values—if not, negotiate for changes until you're comfortable with the terms.

3. The three most dangerous words for an elite athlete: Power of Attorney. This document allows another person legally to become "you." That person can cash your checks, spend your money, and even borrow money in your name without you knowing about it. Someone may ask you to sign a power of attorney "Because then I can pay your bills for you, so you don't need to spend time on that little stuff." **Huge mistake**. There is no reason for you to give up control of your finances, and there is almost never a good reason to sign a power of attorney.

4. Manage your people. If you're a top-level high school or college athlete, you need to talk with your family members to make sure they don't jeopardize your eligibility to play by making illegal deals with agents, boosters, etc. If you're a pro, watch your friends, and make it clear they need to stay out of trouble around you. Having an "entourage" may seem cool, until one of them gets busted for guns or drugs or stealing your money.

5. Get professional help in managing your business affairs. The first two people you should hire are not a driver and a masseuse—they should be your lawyer and your accountant. And don't hire "Uncle Larry's cousin the attorney" either. Find respected professionals who have successfully represented high-level clients for many years.

6. Always pay your taxes. Countless athletes have ended up broke and in legal trouble for not paying their income taxes, and the IRS does not play nice. If you've made it to the pros and you're getting those paychecks, get a professional tax accountant on board to prepare your income tax returns right away.

7. Avoid business deals you can't monitor yourself. The minute you start getting paid, people will start offering you all sorts of "investment opportunities"—most of which are just black holes that will make your money disappear. Forget about real estate deals in Costa Rica or starting a restaurant you'll never actually eat in yourself. Unless you are familiar with the business and have time to keep track of it regularly, just leave your money in the bank until you find investments that make sense for you.

8. Plan for your financial future. The average professional athlete's career is less than three years. No matter how talented you are, you must realize that someday your playing career will come to an end—and it may happen sooner than you expect. If you spend all of the money you make while you're playing, you'll have to start over from scratch when your playing days are over. The first thing you should do with your money: open a retirement account and start saving.

9. Don't overspend. Fancy cars are fun, but they're a huge waste of money. Everybody deserves a nice place to live, but if a house has more bathrooms than you could use in a week, you're better off buying something more modest and keeping the rest of your cash. Think about your money before you spend it; then get what you need without getting crazy.

10. Act like a business owner. Business owners who party every night, blow all their money, and they forget what made them successful in the first place—they go out of business fast. Remember, you are the CEO of "You, Incorporated," and you should handle everything you do in a professional, businesslike manner. While other people are wasting time and money playing the "Big Baller" role, you'll be increasing your success every day.

Always keep in mind: Nobody will care more about your career than you do. It's your responsibility to manage your career well. If you stay focused on your goals and consistently work hard to achieve them, you will naturally find yourself **Standing Above the Crowd**.

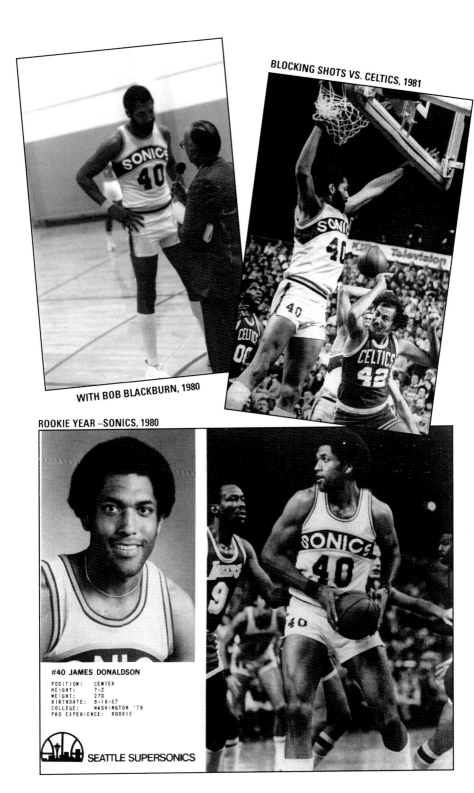

BLOCKING SHOTS VS. CELTICS, 1981

WITH BOB BLACKBURN, 1980

ROOKIE YEAR –SONICS, 1980

#40 JAMES DONALDSON

POSITION: CENTER
HEIGHT: 7-2
WEIGHT: 270
BIRTHDATE: 8-16-57
COLLEGE: WASHINGTON '79
PRO EXPERIENCE: ROOKIE

SEATTLE SUPERSONICS

Sports

WITH WES UNSELD, 1981

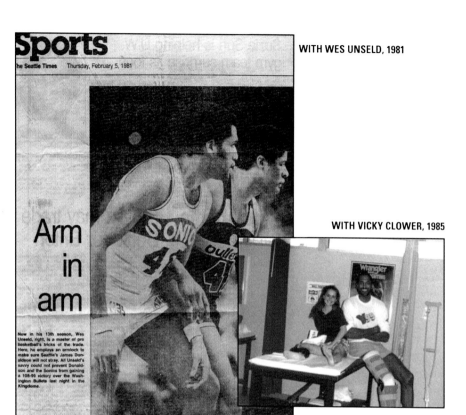

Arm
in
arm

Now in his 13th season, Wes Unseld, right, is a master of pro basketball's tricks of the trade. Here, he employs an armlock to make sure Seattle's James Donaldson will not stray. All Unseld's savvy could not prevent Donaldson and the Sonics from gaining a 108-99 victory over the Washington Bullets last night in the Kingdome.

WITH VICKY CLOWER, 1985

VS. RALPH SAMPSON, 1985

WITH LUKE LONGLEY, 1990

WITH KAREEM ABDUL-JABBAR, 1990'S

WITH TERRY PORTER, 1990's

WITH KURT RAMBIS, 1990's

AS A MAVERICK, CIRCA 1990

WITH MAURICE LUCAS & BRAD DAVIS, 1990's

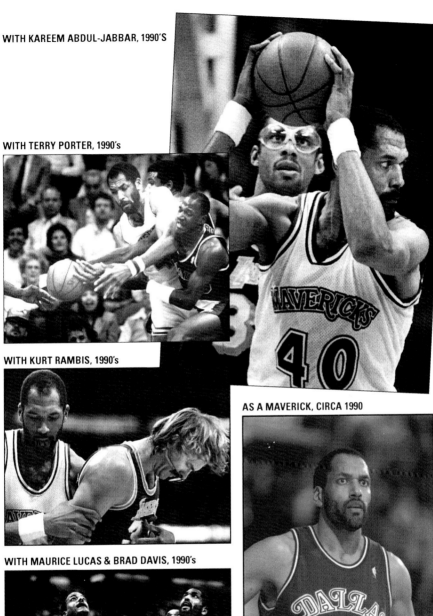

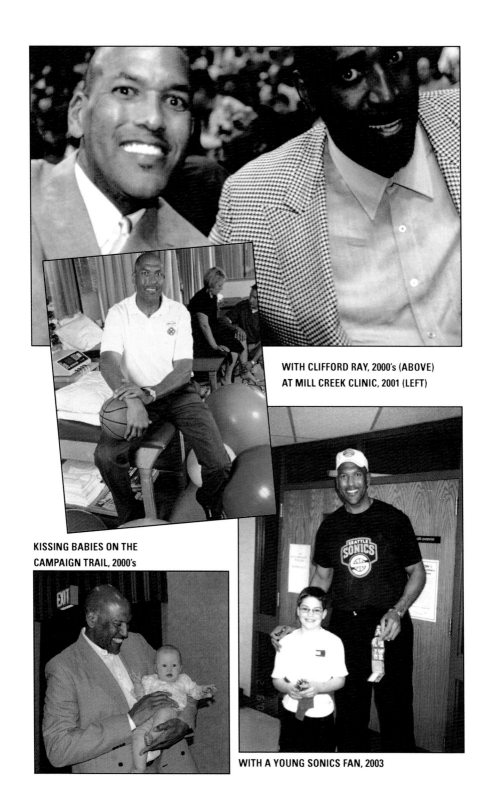

WITH CLIFFORD RAY, 2000's (ABOVE)
AT MILL CREEK CLINIC, 2001 (LEFT)

KISSING BABIES ON THE
CAMPAIGN TRAIL, 2000's

WITH A YOUNG SONICS FAN, 2003

FRIDAY, DECEMBER 31, 2004

WITH TERRELL AT WERLIN
READING PROGRAM, 2006

WITH CLIFFORD RAY, 2007

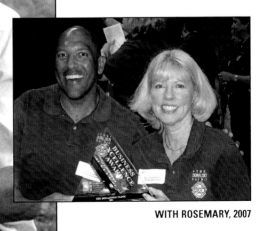

WITH ROSEMARY, 2007

50TH BIRTHDAY, 2007

WITH MANUTE BOL, 2009

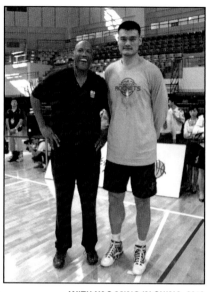

WITH YAO MING IN CHINA, 2010

THE DONALDSON
CLINIC TEAM, 2010

MATT (CENTER) &
DAD (LEFT),
AUGUST 2010

Chapter 12

LIFE IS AN ADVENTURE

Man cannot discover new oceans unless he has
the courage to lose sight of the shore.
— Andre Gide

I have come to realize that the longer I live, the more I learn that there's so much more to learn, do, and see. Famed musician, Roy Ayers has a song titled "Life is Just a Moment," in which he sings about how we need to get out there and enjoy it. I truly believe that because this wonderful experience we all share called "life" goes by so quickly, it's a shame if we don't experience and enjoy it to the fullest.

In this chapter, I'm going to share with you some of the great adventures I've enjoyed in my life, not to show off, but to encourage all of you to get out there and enjoy your lives.

We live in a world that is so fast-paced and high-tech today that I think a lot of us miss out on what it's like to have blades of grass tickle between our toes as we walk barefoot through a meadow. Or simply what it's like to take some time for yourself—just to sit on a park bench and watch the pigeons and squirrels play about.

It's increasingly more and more challenging to get away and find time for yourself; sometimes, you just have to make a concentrated effort to do so. Create your adventures. Don't wait for them to come to you. Adventures can be as simple as finding some "you" time and getting away from everything and everybody. Try spending a couple of hours just relaxing and breathing deeply. Try sitting in a place where you can feel the calming effects of a body of water, be it at the lakeshore, the ocean, beside a pool, or even looking at it from afar.

When we grant ourselves the ability to enjoy this wonderful life, we're all the better for it.

SEVERAL CROSS-COUNTRY ADVENTURES

I've never really considered myself much of an "adventurer" in terms of just wandering off into the woods to see what I can see. I mean, I've had my share of fun observing life, but I've never been the type who needed to climb the highest mountain, swim the deepest sea (I can't swim, anyway), or be there to experience everything firsthand. I applaud those who do, and actually, I'm a little envious of their devil-may-care attitudes. I'm usually content simply to enjoy the world around me.

One adventure I enjoy having on a regular basis is long distance, cross-country driving. There's no better way to get out and experience our great country than to hit the road, especially some of the back roads and "off the beaten paths" that cross our great country.

My home base has been in Seattle since I graduated from Washington State University, but I've had the opportunity to play in other cities around the country and to live and travel overseas.

While playing in the NBA, my first trade (a fact of life for just about every professional athlete) was from the Seattle SuperSonics to the San Diego Clippers in 1983. Since I had quite a few personal belongings (I hadn't quite mastered the art of traveling light) and wanted to take them with me, I just loaded the car, hitched up a U-Haul, and headed south on Interstate 5. It didn't take me long to realize that driving straight on the Interstate would be boring, so that's when I started taking detours and back road adventures. I loved to go off the "beaten path" and drive down the coasts of Oregon and California, enjoying the ocean views and the winding roads throughout the heavily forested parts of the country. The scenery was just breathtaking!

To change it up from time to time, I'd depart from Seattle a week or two early and take the mountain roads through the Sierra Nevada, Cascade, and Rocky Mountain ranges when traveling to other NBA cities that I played in such as Dallas, Salt Lake City, and even New York. NBA basketball season is demanding and draining, but I found that cross-country driving was the best way for me to unwind after the season or to start focusing on the upcoming season. On many occasions, I grabbed a friend or two and said, "Come on; let's hit the road."

Life on the road was always unpredictable because I never knew how far I'd drive on any day, especially if there were some great sites to see along the way. I didn't mind staying in roadside hotels and eating at fast food joints (you can always find a healthy menu item if you try). It's a good thing that I'm a happy-go-lucky, easy-going type because that's how you have to be if you are going to be off the main road.

Unfortunately, that attitude didn't always apply to the people with whom I traveled. I'm the type who doesn't need to check into a hotel if I can catch a quick "cat nap" at a rest stop, but I found out rather quickly that men and women are totally different in that area. When I'd travel with female friends, I learned to slow it down a little and check into a hotel along the way (it might have been for her to keep spruced up more than anything; plus, we could have a little more fun with each other) rather than keep the pedal to the metal, which I would have done when traveling with guy friends. That's okay; I've learned to be versatile, which is an important trait to have if you want to continue growing and being at your best.

In my travels, I would run across folks along the way who would try to put a scare into me from time to time. One day about mid-afternoon when I was driving through a really small town in southern Idaho, I pulled over to get some gas at the only station in town. It was a pretty quiet town where the most exciting activity might have been to sit on the porch and watch the world go by, or to gather at the local fishing hole. As I started to fill up my van, I heard a ruckus. Next, the screeching tires of a pickup truck caught my attention as it skidded to a stop at the gas station. It was loaded with about six or seven guys, who hooted and hollered at me to get out of town because I didn't belong in "these here parts." It took me a split second to finish filling up—all the while keeping an eye on the guys in the pickup less than ten feet away from me—and to hightail it out of town before any trouble broke out. I don't know what would have happened if it had been night, and I didn't want to stick around to find out.

Another time, while driving through and around some Native American reservations in Colorado, my girlfriend and I stopped for the night at a roadside resting place. We woke to find our van surrounded by a dozen or so Native Americans who'd been peering in at us through the windows while we slept. My girlfriend woke up screaming her head off, and I was shocked and scared out of my mind. The Native Americans had formed a circle around the van and were walking around it in circles, slowly and methodically. I don't know whether it was some type of ritual or if they were just trying to scare us, but when you don't know what you need to know, and you're in unfamiliar surroundings, it's best to get the hell out of there—no matter how big and bad you think you might be. I quickly started up the van, and fortunately, got out of there without running any of them over or experiencing any harm myself.

The longest drive I ever completed was from New York City back to Seattle. Now, I know there are more direct routes than what I choose, but that's boring. I took what seemed the longest route possible, driving through Pennsylvania, Virginia, North and South Carolina, Georgia, Alabama, Mississippi, and Arkansas before pulling into Dallas, Texas. Then I headed out through the Southwestern states of New Mexico and Arizona before heading back up north through California and Oregon and finally arriving back in Washington. I can't tell you how many mountain ranges and rivers I've driven across over the years, but some are absolutely breathtaking, such as the coastal routes, Yellowstone National Park, the Grand Canyon, and just about everything else in between.

My longest stretch of driving nonstop was from Chamberlain, South Dakota to Spokane, Washington in one stretch, a distance of almost 1,100 miles. It took me about twenty hours, but with a couple of mega-sized coffees and a few snacks and some good tunes, it was a breeze.

Strange things happen when you're on the road. I remember driving through West Texas, Arizona, and Colorado and being able to look up and out my window to see meteor showers and comets on nights when the sky was clear and star-filled. On occasion, I thought my eyes were playing tricks on me; I could have sworn more than once that I saw what looked like a UFO. Not that I know what a UFO is supposed to look like, but I do know that stars and comets aren't supposed to light up the night and dart willy-nilly across the sky.

The strangest occurrence I ever had on a road trip was seeing what I believe to have been a Sasquatch or Bigfoot. No lie!

I was on a small highway in eastern Oregon in broad daylight. Mine was the only car for what seemed like miles around. As I was coming down the highway and going at a good clip of about eighty miles an hour, I looked up, and about 100 yards or so ahead of me, dashing across the road, was what I swear had to be Bigfoot.

Now, this happened in broad daylight and I was fully rested (and keep in mind that I don't drink, smoke, or do drugs, so I was in my "right mind"). I was driving a big Dodge maxivan, fully outfitted with a mini-fridge, sink, television, and a great stereo system. Two of my favorite dogs, Jazzi and Rico, were stretched out in the back, comfortably resting on the couch.

Being a tall guy myself, I know what a seven- to eight-foot object looks like. When you're my height, unless you want to knock yourself silly by constantly hitting your head, you need to have a good sense of space and the dimensions of objects around you, including knowing that the average doorway is "only" 6'8" tall!

As I got closer to what I believed to be Bigfoot, I figured he had to be at least eight feet tall! I'm taller than my van, and this creature was much taller than my van! He was walking upright rather rapidly, and by the time I got to the point of the road where he was, he was disappearing into the brush. I wanted to stop and turn around to look at what I saw, but I thought better of it and kept on going. It really got my heart racing, though, because it was unlike anything I'd ever seen.

One of the drawbacks and ironic things about going on adventures is that many times you come back with hard-to-believe stories. Everyone gets a good chuckle out of my Bigfoot story, but anyone who knows me and hears the anxiety in my voice when I talk about it knows I must've seen something on the back roads of eastern Oregon.

I have a friend in Seattle who loves to go out on his small fishing boat, and invariably, he comes back with some stories of his own. He's told me stories about everything from flying fish to beautiful mermaids. According to him, one mermaid actually climbed into the boat with him and they had a conversation. I do keep in mind that my friend likes to have a couple of twelve-packs on board with him (that come home empty!), so I take his stories with a grain of salt and a smile. I only wish I'd had a video camera ready to go when I saw Bigfoot. You'll just have to take my word for it.

TRAVELING TO SOUTH AFRICA

In 2003, I joined a group of more than 100 people from my home church, Mount Zion Baptist Church in Seattle, for a trip to our church's sister city in Port Elizabeth, South Africa. We traveled there not only as part of a great adventure, but also to help dedicate a new church building we were partly financing.

I knew most of the people who traveled to South Africa with the group, so it was an enjoyable but long trip. It was my first trip to the continent of Africa and I'm glad I was able to be part of the contingency that traveled there.

One of the things that jumped out at me during my trip to South Africa was the huge distinction between the "haves" and the "have-nots," the rich and the poor, and the black and the white. You hear stories and see documentaries from time to time, but nothing can take the place of experiencing South Africa firsthand. We walked through shantytowns and went to Robben Island, where freedom fighter, and former South African president, Nelson Mandela, was imprisoned for twenty-seven years. The prison and jail cell have been kept in the same condition as when Mandela served his time there, and your imagination can't help but take off when the tour guide tells you about how severe conditions were for Mandela and his fellow prisoners.

The prison, made mostly of stone and concrete, was very drab and dreary. We were shown where prisoners were held in isolation and where they were made to break rocks and stones in the gravel pits. We saw what amounted to a "play yard" where the prisoners could be outside to get some fresh air for a few minutes a day under the watchful eyes of heavily armed prison guards. What really caught my attention was how few comforts of home (TV, recreation rooms, air conditioning, etc.) were available, and that the prisoners were made to feel miserable. Prisoners here in the United States have it easy compared to what we saw at Robben Island.

During our visit, we traveled for two weeks on chartered buses between Johannesburg, Cape Town, Port Elizabeth, and East London. Everyone behaved well for the most part, but you always have one or two folks who "get on everyone's nerves." I think the fact that we were a "church group" helped in that regard. You just find yourself saying a little prayer and praying that the annoyance will somehow go away. I'm pretty skilled at not showing someone that he might be getting on my nerves, but not everyone is that way. I just say to myself that those people aren't going to spoil my fun!

After arriving in South Africa, we had an opportunity to enjoy the ocean views of Cape Town. It's a beautiful sight from high up in the cliffs to look down to where the Indian and Atlantic Oceans converge. We were surrounded by baboons that had lost any fear of humans. They were an intimidating presence to us as we got off the bus. The baboons weren't shy at all about snatching purses or grabbing bags and then running off into the bushes with them. So it wasn't unusual to hear someone scream when a baboon stole something, or to hear a child cry when the baboons walked, or ran, right up to them and grabbed food out of their hands. Some of those baboons were good-sized (about the size of a small human) and weighed about 70 to 100 pounds. It's rumored they have super strength, so you don't want to play around with them

One of the highlights of our trip was an African safari. It almost didn't take place because our group spent a little too much time at the dedication service for the new church building. Our hosts wanted us to stay longer than we'd anticipated, so in order to get to the safari, we needed to leave right after the church service since it was already 1 or 2 p.m. We actually had a split among our group since some wanted to stay and continue enjoying the dedication service that was going on far too long, and others (myself in particular), wanted to head out toward the safari. We had use of three chartered buses for our trip, so I talked our group organizer into letting us have one of the buses so we could head toward the safari. He put up some resistance, but I think he could tell he was going to have some big problems on his hands if he didn't relent. We had a long trip ahead of us (about four hours), so we had to get going in a hurry. That didn't go over well with our group organizer, but I stood up and spoke for those of us who were going, even if it meant I'd have to drive the bus myself! Our group organizer saw we were serious and determined to head off to the safari, with or without his approval. Besides, what could he do? We were way out in the middle of South Africa. He realized he had a determined, frustrated, and soon to be angry group on his hands. We all agreed that none of us had traveled this far so we could miss out on the opportunity to see an African safari.

Well, we made it to the safari and enjoyed watching some of the most magnificent beasts in their natural state. We saw elephants that seemed to be as large as our charter bus. We saw hippopotamuses, rhinos, zebras, gazelles, giraffes, and lions. It was indeed the trip of a lifetime. I felt bad for those who stayed behind and missed out.

Another enjoyable experience was going to an authentic "African Village," complete with "villagers" in full African dress, with food, dance, and music to boot! I was picked by the villagers to be a ceremonial African King, and they brought out several beautiful robes and trinkets and outfitted me with them so that I very much looked the part. My size and height cause a great deal of commotion everywhere I go, but that really kicked into high gear during our visit to the village. It was fun and a great experience.

ADAPTING TO LIFE IN OTHER COUNTRIES

I've been fortunate to travel the world and experience different cultures, people, and lifestyles. When I travel to other countries, I try to adapt as much as I can. We've all heard the term, "Ugly American" in reference to the person from the United States who gives the rest of us a bad reputation. Whether that reputation is deserved or not, we all need to be on our best behavior and make sure we leave a good impression with the rest of the world.

Other than being born in England (because my father was in the Air Force) and coming back to the States when I was two years old, my first time overseas was when I was a student athlete at Washington State University and our team traveled to Yugoslavia to participate in a basketball tournament. I was happy for the opportunity to go, and I learned that even though people are different, speak different languages, and have different cultures, we're all pretty much the same. Athletic competition is universal, as we see in the Olympic Games that are played every four years in one of the participant countries. Countries support their sports teams and root them on to victory through the spirit of athletic competition.

What I like most about traveling is experiencing other food and different cultures. When I visited Yugoslavia, I wasn't a vegetarian yet, so I tried just about anything that was put in front of me, as long as I could identify it or have someone tell me what I was eating. I'm not too crazy about trying exotic foods that are way outside of the mainstream, but I did experience a wide variety of food and cuisine from around the world.

In Yugoslavia, I had my first experience with bread that didn't look or taste like the bread I knew. I grew up on the childhood favorite "Wonder Bread," and I feasted regularly on peanut butter and jelly sandwiches. But in Yugoslavia, I was given my first taste of bread that was as hard as rock on the outside and almost tasteless on the inside. I used to slather it down in tasteless butter and find some jelly or honey to put on it just so I could deal with it. But as with most things, I learned that if you approach "newness and change" with an open mind, then it's so much easier to "deal with it." I grew to love the breads throughout Europe, and after a while, I noticed that the American breads were the ones really lacking in taste.

ITALY

The next time I went overseas was as a graduate from Washington State University. The Seattle SuperSonics drafted me in 1979, but I didn't know the first thing about NBA basketball at the time in terms of what adjustments would be required, so I thought I was good enough to be on the team. However, my agent convinced me that the best road to the NBA would first involve a stop in Italy for me to hone my skills.

So instead of turning out for the SuperSonics, where I would have most likely been cut because I wasn't yet good enough (plus the Sonics were coming off of the championship season, so they were fully loaded with great players), I headed to Siena, Italy for my first season of professional basketball. My mindset was "NBA or bust," but the reality was that I needed to go to Italy to start perfecting my skills. There, I would get the playing experience I wouldn't get sitting on the bench in the NBA. I went kicking and screaming, not really understanding why my agent insisted I take that route, but once I settled down and got into a routine, I realized it wasn't going to be so bad.

Playing professional sports overseas has a well-deserved reputation for not working out too well for those who choose to do it. My advice? Get paid as much as you can upfront! Sure, athletes get a chance to play, and they are paid well compared to the country's "home-grown" talent. Unfortunately, imported athletes are usually shortchanged—referred to as "leaving some money on the table," which means that even though your contact calls for a certain amount for you to be paid, mysteriously, especially as the team comes down the home stretch and prepares for the playoffs, the team owners will say they're having financial challenges and that they aren't going to be able to pay you. You can try to sue them (I tried that twice) if you want, but good luck with that.

I played a total of six years overseas, and each year I "left money on the table." My first year in Siena was no exception. I was a green and rawboned rookie, just fresh out of college, so I encountered what most college players do as they embark upon their careers overseas. Basketball fans overseas are so enamored with NBA players that anybody who lacks NBA experience is in for a rough time, no matter how well he plays. Fans have a mindset that just about any NBA castoff is better than a college kid who's never played in the NBA. So, even though a non-NBA player might be playing well and doing what's expected of him (and her nowadays), fans want a player with professional experience. Consequently, my initial fan club was small.

Not long after I arrived in Siena, my coach and team management started going back and forth about how the fans wanted a player with NBA experience. I was young and still learning the game, but for the most part, I was a productive player. I was able to score, rebound, and play defense, but perhaps not with the NBA flair, and definitely without the NBA pedigree that my team and fans wanted. Right before the guaranteed date (typically a date in September before the regular season begins in which all contracts become guaranteed), I heard a knock on my apartment door. It was my basketball coach. He told me the team could no longer use me and I was free to go. I had a guaranteed contract for the whole year, but that didn't mean a thing. The team no longer needed my services. I was free, actually *strongly encouraged,* to head back to the States.

The team had obtained the services of an NBA journeyman, Ron Behagen, and essentially ripped up my contract right under my nose. All I could do was call my agent to ask for his advice. My agent was in Pasadena, California and I was way over in Siena, Italy, unable to speak the language and not knowing a soul except my teammates. My agent advised me to hang in there and not leave the team or the city because then it could be deemed that I had walked out of my contract. So I stayed in Siena from September 1979 until Easter Day 1980.

The Siena team tried to entice me to leave by agreeing to pay a percentage of what it owed me, but I stuck to my guns and hung in there. That was tough, especially when the holidays rolled around. It was no fun spending Thanksgiving, Christmas, New Year's, and Valentine's Day in a foreign place with very few friends at the time and family so far away.

I ended up going to an Italian court with a couple of Italian lawyers every other week from September to April until we were finally able to reach a settlement. Then I was free to go.

The biggest difficulty was that I could no longer practice or travel with the team. I went to games on occasion, but it was bittersweet and I didn't enjoy it after a while. Behagen, the NBA journeyman, and I became friends and I hung with him and his family, but there wasn't much joy in that either, knowing he'd taken my place on the team. I did make friends with several families in Siena, learned to speak the language fluently, and overall, tried to make the best of the situation.

I share this story so you will see that no matter what situation you're in, there's always a bright side to it. Many of us travel for pleasure and for fun and things go well. Others choose to work overseas, or go to school overseas. Whatever the reason you travel, make the best of the situation and don't hide away from the experience or fight it. Make friends, enjoy the people, food, music and culture, and you'll find yourself happier and much better off.

Today, I'm glad things worked out the way they did because I made friends in Siena who are still dear friends today. I became fluent in a beautiful language, learned the history and culture of Italy, and of course, ate up a storm of great Italian cooking.

Carlo and Carla Pasqui and their young daughter, Viviana, were among the "adopted families" who took me in while I was in Siena and left me with some great memories. Carlo was a great basketball fan who knew I was caught up in a bad contract situation with the Siena team. One day, he invited me over to his house to meet his wife and daughter. Pretty soon, I was at their house just about every day. In the early days, none of them spoke English, and we communicated by drawing simple pictures—especially in regards to what we might be eating that day. We'd draw chickens, roosters, pigs, rabbits, squirrels, and sparrows—at least, I think they were sparrows! On occasion, we'd draw a cow's tongue or a bull's balls to describe what was on the menu. It was humorous at times, as we found ourselves playing games, charades, and drawing—whatever it took to communicate. Fortunately, it only took me a matter of weeks to get a handle on the language, and soon, I communicated in nearly flawless Italian.

Carla was a fantastic cook and she cooked every meal we had—be it breakfast, lunch, or dinner. On many occasions, I was there for all three! Carla was a typical Italian housewife who wanted you to eat everything she put in front of you and actually took it personally if you didn't eat it. "Mangia, mangia!" she would say, meaning "Eat, eat!", and that's what I did! I would eat everything in front of me, and after I finished eating, Carla would go back in the kitchen and proudly pull another tray of food out of the oven and we'd all begin again. Unfortunately, my dear friend Carlo passed away several years after I left Siena, but I stayed in touch with him until he passed. I'm still in touch with Carla and Viviana, and they remain dear friends, even though they still don't speak a word of English.

SPAIN

After I returned to the States from Italy, I promptly went on a couple of barnstorming tours to see whether I could enhance my opportunities of getting a contract, either overseas or with the NBA. Seeing I'd hardly played at all in Siena because of my contract dispute, I hadn't gotten an opportunity to develop my skills much past the level they were when I went to Siena in the first place.

I decided then, before leaving for the U.S., to tour Italy with a group of basketball players during the summer of 1980. We had a lot of fun going from town to town to play at outdoor venues against local professional and semi-pro teams. We usually played in small, out of the way towns, where it was a big community event to have a professional basketball game played.

Summers in Mediterranean countries can be unbearably hot, so it was common to play outside on portable courts with bleachers all around. My team members and I were all desperate to land jobs, so we had a lot of competition between us and there wasn't much camaraderie on the court, meaning there was a lot of "selfish running and gunning" as we tried to show off our skills to basketball officials and scouts who might be in the stands. We still won the vast majority of our games though, because we were much better and talented players than our competition.

John Fultz was one of my favorite team members during that time. John had played professional basketball in Europe for several years by the time I got there, and he was still a very good player, even though he was toward the end of his career. He played the forward position and had outstanding skills shooting the ball from inside and out. Together, we got the nickname "Thunder and Lightning" because he was deadly from outside, shooting the ball from every imaginable spot on the court, and I dominated inside by dunking the ball, blocking shots, and intimidating players. We had a great time, and he taught me a lot of the rules of living overseas and dealing with just about every situation that comes up. John never got a chance to play in the NBA, but he was as good a shooter as anybody I've seen.

After that tour in 1980, I returned to Seattle to try out for the SuperSonics. The Sonics still had my draft rights, meaning I was not able to negotiate or talk to any other NBA team unless the Sonics either released or traded me. I ended up making the Sonics and played my first three NBA seasons there.

After playing fourteen years in the NBA with teams such as the Sonics, Clippers, Mavericks, Knicks, and Jazz, I went back overseas to Spain in

1993 and played for a team in Seville. As athletes age, they discover not only that their athletic skills start fading, but also, the demand for their services fades just as quickly, if not even quicker.

I found that the demand for my services was fading quickly, but I still had a strong desire to continue playing basketball. If you're going to have any kind of "market value" to a prospective team, you've got to stay sharp and be seen competing on a regular basis and at high level.

I chose to return to Europe and play for a team in Spain mainly because I was hoping to be picked up by an NBA team during the mid-season or whenever I could, plus the Spanish basketball league was considered one of the most competitive at the time. The NBA probably will always be the pinnacle of professional basketball, and once you reach the top, it seems like nothing else will do, but that didn't mean I didn't want to keep playing.

Since I was born in England, I was able to play as a European National, which meant I belonged to the European Community and had a dual passport. So, I was able to play on European professional teams as a European National and utilize my dual citizenship. The European basketball leagues have a limit of two foreign players per team. The "foreign players" are most always American-born with American passports. By using my dual citizenship, the team could acquire two more American players without jeopardizing the team's quota. The team we fielded in Seville was probably the most star-studded team in the entire European professional basketball league at the time.

I had a wonderful time in Seville, one of the most beautiful cities in the world. The weather there was outstanding most of the year, and the women were just gorgeous. I had a nice apartment in Seville in a complex that housed several neighbors who became my good friends. I was always over at their homes, visiting and enjoying a meal, and I am still friends with them years later. Seville remains my favorite European city to this day.

I think the reason I get along so well in every situation is because I choose to. So many of my teammates from the U.S. chose not to get involved with the local people, which I think is a mistake. I feel that as an American it's my role to be a goodwill ambassador to people when I visit their countries. A lot of resentment exists among the people in some of the countries where I've lived because of American foreign politics, and when Americans visit those countries and play the "Ugly American" role, it doesn't help one bit. For the most part, people around the world admire Americans and want to emulate much of our lifestyle, so we're already at an advantage to be accepted into their cultures. Therefore, we should do our best to build positive relationships and create "win-win" situations everywhere we go.

GREECE

In 1994, after Seville, I played in Thessaloniki, Greece. During that time, I still had hopes and dreamed about returning to the NBA because I didn't feel my career there was over yet. But I kept a positive attitude and took basketball opportunities wherever I could. My dream when I started my professional basketball career was to be the first player ever to play twenty years in the NBA. It didn't quite come to fruition as I had hoped it would since six of those years were overseas, but I still got to play professional basketball for twenty years.

My stay in Greece was a little more challenging than the time I spent in Italy and Spain. Also, I found that learning the Greek language was more difficult than learning Italian or Spanish, but I wanted to learn, so I dove right in.

I remember meeting the neighbors in my apartment complex as I sat outside one night, enjoying a veggie gyro sandwich. It must have been the first week or so after I arrived in Thessaloniki. It was a warm summer night, and I'd arrived to get ready for the season. I was sitting out by the curb, when before I knew it, a couple of young boys pointed me out and walked toward me. Now, people point me out everywhere I go, but these two youngsters were interested in having a conversation with me. It was obvious they were basketball fans, and they knew who I was. It turned out that I lived in the apartment just a couple of floors below them. The older boy, Aris, (sixteen at the time), spoke a little bit of English, and I understood him well enough to have a conversation. His younger brother, Ilias (twelve at the time), was a little shy and could barely speak a word of English, but he tagged along everywhere Aris went. They invited me up to their apartment to meet their mother, father, and the rest of the family (grandfather, grandmother, aunt, etc.). Before long, we were fast friends, and they helped me learn the language. I never quite mastered it, but I became adept at conversational Greek. The Greeks, much like my Italian and Spanish friends, were hospitable and insisted that I come by to share a meal with them just about every day. My motto after awhile became, "For a meal…I'll be there!"

I'm constantly asked which country where I played I enjoyed the best. I break it down like this. For lifestyle, pace of living, and just enjoying life, I feel Spain was the best place for that. In regards to being a tourist and seeing some of the most magnificent cathedrals, plazas, and a rich, romantic history, I felt Italy was the best place for me. As far as basketball competition, it was Greece.

I try to return to the Mediterranean countries where I played every two or three years, and I maintain friendships with people I met while living there. The adventures and life experiences I had in those countries taught me how to adapt in every situation I encountered and to deal and communicate with people everywhere I go. Here in Seattle, I've made friends with people from communities in Eastern and Western Africa, and many friends from Southeastern Asia. I love the opportunities to learn and to share and understand the differences that exist between people. I have discovered that we can always find ways to speak universal languages through sports, body language, smiles, and breaking bread together.

I encourage each of you to extend a hand to those who are little different from you. Have an open mind and open ears to hear and understand— from *another person's* point of view.

One of my early introductions to politics was when I lived overseas. Friends who live in those countries pointed out the "ugly underbelly of American politics." They told me how our political system had affected their lives and built resentment. In 1994, I was in Thessaloniki when there was a lot of disagreement about whether Macedonia belonged to Greece or Albania. The Greek people were outraged that the United States imposed its will upon the U.N. to have Macedonia go to Albania. I was in my hotel room, five or six floors above the city, when a throng of about 200,000 people lined the streets and shouted, "Down with America" and burned an effigy of President Bill Clinton. So, I'm very serious when I talk about how politics affect people in the U.S. and other nations.

SUMMARY

Your journey in life zips by so fast that you're at the end of it before you know it. Seek adventure, get outside your comfort zone, and live life to the fullest. Not only will having such experiences get you out of your comfort zone, but they will build confidence in you so you can **Stand Above the Crowd**. Besides, such experiences are great fun once you allow yourself to have fun. So many things are available to enjoy in life and so many adventures exist that we can embrace with gusto. Being a well-rounded and well-versed person will only enrich your life and your outlook on the world. When you share experiences with people who are outside of your normal circle, you quickly realize the world is such a big place and you have so many reasons to be grateful.

When you travel, go off the beaten path. Interact with folks you wouldn't normally speak with, or who hardly speak English and rarely get a chance to see Americans up close and personal. Your life and perspective will be richer, fuller, and lasting. You can visit tourist traps anytime, but when you have a chance to enjoy authentic experiences, embrace them.

Whether traveling to the countryside or across the sea, go with an open mind, eyes, and heart, and you'll be amazed at what you can learn from the world around you.

Chapter 13

WHAT SPARKED THE DONALDSON CLINIC

It was March 3, 1989. I was starting center for the Dallas Mavericks in a game against the Houston Rockets at the Summit in Houston, Texas. I was matched against one of the all-time greats, Hakeem Olajuwon. Since he was one of the best centers around and known to give me fits in trying to guard him, I always tried to psych myself up to be a little more energetic and alert than usual when I played against him. Psyching yourself up is something you do when you compete against the best. You realize your competition may have a physical advantage over you, so it becomes a mind game in which you have to psych yourself up to be better than you typically are.

We were four minutes into the game. I was going up for an offensive rebound when I felt myself crumple to the hardwood. At first, I didn't realize what had happened, but a split second later, I felt a tremendous pain sear through my right leg. It happened in just a moment or two. I saw myself falling to the ground, seemingly in slow motion. In the time it actually took me to hit the ground, I realized something was terribly wrong with my knee.

Going into the game, I'd had problems with my right knee, a severe case of tendinitis. Being an athlete, I was accustomed to playing in pain.

Throughout the season, I'd been getting painkilling medication, cortisone shots, anti-inflammatories, lots of ice, and as much rest as I could get between games and practice. I was the kind of guy who'd play no matter what. I'd tell the doc and trainers to, "Wrap me up and give me what I need so I can keep playing." They obliged me, mainly because I really wanted to continue playing, but also because the team invests heavily in its athletes and keeps the pressure on the medical professionals to get us back out there as quickly as possible. I learned later that I shouldn't have been taking all the medications and the shots, but I wanted to bear my share of the responsibility and push myself to the maximum.

From the moment I went up for that offensive rebound to the moment I ended up in a crumpled heap on the floor of the Summit, I knew something was terribly wrong. I lay flat on my back for a few seconds, and by that time, the pain had become unbearable. I looked down at my right knee and I could see that my kneecap had retracted up to about mid-thigh. There was no way I could get to my feet by my own power. Within a few seconds, my teammates and several guys on the other team were helping me up because they could see I was in pain. I never did quite make it all the way back onto my feet because they laid me on a stretcher. It took about six or eight guys to lift me and carry me back to the locker room. One of the things we learn quickly as professional athletes is "The show must go on," so before I had even made it into the locker room, play had resumed on the court. In the locker room, the medical professionals gave me a quick evaluation of what was going on. They could tell something was terribly wrong with my knee—so could I.

We decided to get me back to Dallas as quickly as possible, where a team doctor would be waiting to evaluate my injury. It turned out I had a ruptured patella tendon in my right knee, and it was severe. Within a couple of days, I was undergoing surgery to have my patella tendon re-connected. The patella tendon is the main tendon that runs over the top of and alongside the kneecap. It's instrumental in allowing one to stop and start, jump, twist and spin…all the things basketball players must be able to do. It was a rare injury, and the doctors said they had never seen one as severe. They told me that my patella tendon resembled a "bowl of spaghetti," and that the tendon was shredded and would need to be carefully reconstructed. Doctors being doctors, they were guarded in any kind of prognosis that would give me hopes of a full recovery so I could continue as a professional athlete. In fact, the doctors were full of doom and gloom, even though they tried to hide it from me as best they could. They didn't know if I'd ever be able to walk without a limp, let alone become a world-class athlete again.

I had no idea what a long road to recovery lay ahead of me, and looking back, I'm glad I didn't; if I'd known all the work full recovery would entail, I'm not sure I would have been able to pull myself together to do it.

THE RECOVERY

Other than some basic minor injuries from time to time (sprained ankles, pulled muscles, strained back, etc.), I didn't know a whole lot about physical therapy or what physical therapists did. Athletic teams, from high school to the pros, are accustomed to having athletic trainers at practice and games to help players with minor bumps and bruises. All major college and professional teams have a team doctor who attends most of the practices and all games to keep an eye on the players and attend to any injuries that may occur. When a player sustains a serious injury, the doctor is quick to run from the stands or sidelines to assist the player. As I mentioned earlier, athletes are huge investments (at the college and professional levels) to the teams, so they want to protect their investment as much as possible.

Most athletes are very competitive by nature, so when they receive an injury, you almost have to drag them off the field or off the court, kicking and screaming. The competitive athletes almost make an oath to themselves that there is no way they'll leave unless they're carried out. That's a little extreme, because many times athletes push themselves beyond their limits, which can have detrimental effects on their overall health. I'm glad to see that the college and professional ranks are starting to pay more attention to athletic injuries, and especially to a new classification of injuries: concussion and brain injuries. You don't see concussion and brain injuries too often in baseball and basketball, track and field, and the like, but you will see them quite often in football. Currently, the NFL is conducting a study on concussions and brain injuries, and several NFL players have volunteered to participate in these scientific studies, which can only result in a better understanding of them and how to prevent as well as heal such injuries.

The road to recovery from my patella tendon injury was long and tedious. For the first three or four weeks, I didn't do much other than have a full-length lightweight cast placed on my leg. I was ordered to stay off it, and I had to use crutches even to scoot around the kitchen and the living room. Have you ever seen crutches built for a 7'2" guy? The crutches I had (and still have…just in case) are at least 5½ to 6 feet tall, and there's no way a person of normal height could ever get any use out of them except perhaps as a pole vaulting apparatus!

I probably wasn't a model patient because I always seemed to push myself just a little more than what made my doctors comfortable. I don't recommend doing that to anyone, but I was stubborn; I recall riding my bicycle around the neighborhood with my right leg in a full-length lightweight cast, and pedaling with my left leg. I'm sure it was a remarkable sight, and I was "oh so careful" not to hit any potholes or curbs while I was riding. The most difficult part was starting and stopping. But once I got going and got the hang of it, I was pretty good.

Another thing that I returned to before my doctors felt I was ready was getting involved with martial arts (tae kwon do) again. Of course, I was careful not to overdo it, but doctors tend to take a cautionary path when it comes to getting patients back on their feet again. I don't blame them, because many things can go wrong, and of course, most people would blame the doctor instead of themselves. In my case, I was fully prepared to take responsibility for anything I did wrong, so I was very careful in speeding my way back to recovery.

One near-tragic episode happened when I was just returning to my jogging routine several months after my surgery. I was out jogging with my dogs through some hillsides. One of the dogs cut across the pathway right at my feet before I could react to him, and down I went, landing on both knees and skidding across the gravel. I knew for sure that something was going to be broken, but miraculously, other than a few scrapes and a little blood, I was fine. I was scared out of my wits, but I was fine!

THE INSPIRATION FOR THE DONALDSON CLINIC

Anyone who has gone through physical therapy knows that the time in rehabilitation seems to pass super slowly. First, there's almost always the traumatic situation that got you into physical therapy in the first place (automobile accident, falling down a flight of stairs, throwing your back out, etc.), and the pain associated with it. Sure, there's pain from the injury and/or surgery, but there's also the pain the physical therapist is likely to cause (not purposefully, though...I don't think) in the process of getting the injured area to respond to treatment and exercise. I call physical therapy almost inevitable today since people are living longer and are more active than ever. Now, along with death and taxes, there is physical therapy. Even if you skate along scot-free throughout life, if you live long enough, you will wear out your joints and most likely have them replaced, and then, you'll have to undergo physical therapy.

As I went through weeks and months of physical rehabilitation, I realized I had gone from being one of the strongest, roughest, and toughest NBA players to a patient flat on his back. Simple movements, such as leg raises with a three-pound weight on my leg, challenged me. I was fortunate to have a great team of therapists, athletic trainers, and doctors working with me throughout my physical rehab. They encouraged me to get back to full strength and function again. My injury was not common and few of the professional athletes with that injury had ended their careers or had their ability to perform be hampered, but I still took to my physical therapy like a duck to water because I didn't want to leave anything to chance. I pushed myself as hard as I could to return to my full performance level as quickly as possible.

During this time, I befriended a young girl who was also going to physical therapy. Vicky Clower was a fourteen-year-old athlete who had just suffered a serious knee injury while skiing. I remember how pleasant she was and how she had such an optimistic and upbeat personality. It was contagious, and as we became friends, she continually encouraged me to keep pushing myself throughout my physical therapy. As the weeks wore on, Vicky and I made physical therapy as much fun and enjoyable as possible. Her mom, Sharon, brought in cookies and baked goods for the whole staff, which helped to make the whole experience uplifting. We must have been a funny duo—the big, powerful NBA player, and the sweet and innocent child who, through her encouragement, helped an NBA player back to being an athlete again.

Twenty years later, Vicky and I are still in touch. When I told her I would mention her in this book, she became shy and self-conscious about it. I know, however, without her positive encouragement, my journey back would have been much more difficult—if not impossible.

During my physical therapy and rehab, I had what you would call a "light-bulb moment" where I thought, "If I can't ever return to playing basketball again, what in the world am I going to do?" That is when I had the inspiration to start up my own physical therapy clinic. I knew at that moment that if I never returned to basketball, the next chapter in my career would be either as a physical therapist or as the owner/operator of a physical therapy clinic. I wanted to establish a wonderful physical therapy clinic that would provide a positive, uplifting environment for patients who were going through an ordeal similar to what I had gone through.

The Donaldson Clinic began shortly after I finished my physical therapy rehab in 1989. I remember talking to my agent at the time and mentioning that it was what I wanted to do with my life at that point. He knew a young upstart physical therapist from the Seattle area who was in physical therapy school in Southern California with his daughter; that person became the first player on my team. I didn't know then that I would return to play professional basketball for another ten years; all I knew was that I wanted to be proactive and have a backup plan in case I couldn't return to professional basketball. It's the advice I give to all young athletes, whether they're going through a traumatic experience or not—have a backup plan. You never know how your athletic endeavors will turn out so always be prepared.

In 2010, The Donaldson Clinic celebrated its twentieth-year anniversary. From day one, I've had the same operations manager, Rosemary Bennetts, as the mainstay and stabilizing force. If I could grant one wish to all small business operators out there, it would be to find an outstanding team member and person like Rosemary Bennetts has been for us at The Donaldson Clinic.

The Donaldson Clinic has become my life after being a professional athlete, and I'm glad I started it when I did. I could never have just retired and sat around after my professional career, and it allows me to remain involved in athletics in another way. Not only did it become a backup plan, but it led me in new directions discovering more of my potential and the possibilities life has to offer as an entrepreneur.

Chapter 14

ADVICE FOR WOULD-BE SMALL BUSINESS ENTREPRENEURS

As a kid, I was afraid of "business." Because I steered clear of business courses in high school and college, I graduated from college knowing little, if anything, about what business is all about.

How many of us are like that? We steer around obstacles and challenges that scare us. When we look back years later, however, we see there wasn't much to be afraid of, other than, as President Franklin D. Roosevelt so eloquently put it, "fear itself."

When I was growing up, very few businesspeople were in my community. My mother and my father weren't businesspeople, and as I think back, I can't come up with anybody I really knew back then who was a business-person. I can probably count on one hand the number of businesspeople I came across during my childhood in Sacramento.

That's the way it is for many young people. They don't get to experi-ence different lifestyles/career choices and see things beyond what they're exposed to in their immediate surroundings. I work with several young people who have never even ventured outside their neighborhoods. I know many who haven't even been to downtown Seattle, even though they live only a ten minute bus ride away. So for me to grow up in a neighborhood where I didn't see any businesspeople, well, that was par for the course. It's another reason why we have to emphasize the value of an education to our young people and make sure they get an opportunity to experience life and all it has to offer.

I didn't get interested in business until I had the vision of operating my own business shortly after my devastating knee injury in 1988. I didn't know the first thing about what it would take to get something like that started. All I knew was that it was what I wanted to do. I was going to seek out the best people I knew in my limited world of business experience, so I could make it happen.

Like most people, I turned to my family to see whether they knew anyone I could talk to, but not surprisingly, they didn't know anyone. Next I turned to my agent at the time, Don DeJardin, and he helped me to envision what owning a business would look and feel like, as well as doing my homework to find out how to make it happen. Once I narrowed it down to knowing I wanted to own a physical therapy center where I could provide the same outstanding physical therapy services I'd received as a Dallas Maverick, Don helped me to put the ball in motion. As I said before, he helped me connect with a physical therapy student who became the start of my team.

The first task when starting a business is to round up the resources that will help you fulfill your dream. Who's going to be on your team? What resources will you need? What experience/skills do you lack that you'll need to improve? Can you gain those skills by furthering your education? Will your team's skills make up the difference in areas where you're currently weak?

I'm the first to admit that when I began, I knew nothing about business. Therefore, I began by rounding up the team members who could compensate and excel in areas where I was lacking. A great shortcoming of many small business entrepreneurs is they think they can do it all, so they try to wear every hat. Running a business requires you to take a good look at what you can and cannot do on your own. Ask yourself, "Am I good at accounting? Do I understand legal documents and contracts? Who's going to prepare my taxes?" The list goes on and on.

My team background came into play during this process. When I played on basketball teams, I played the position of center. I never pretended to be the point guard. Sure, once in a blue moon, I could throw the ball up there and hit from half court, but that wasn't my job, and it wasn't going to benefit my team and enhance our chances of winning. For NBA trivia buffs, if anyone asks you who played the most number of seasons and games without attempting a three-point shot, the answer is me! I knew my job, my strengths, and how to help my team. My job was to stay down in the trenches and battle for rebounds, play defense, and jam home a few offensive rebounds. When you start your business, know your strengths, know your weaknesses, know who you want to add to your team, and what role everyone is going to play.

The first people on my team as I started my physical therapy business were my agent, Don DeJardin, my corporate and personal attorney, Dave Ellenhorn, my corporate and personal CPA, Colin Brine, followed years later by another corporate and personal CPA, George Stewart, and my financial advisor, Sylvia Parker. That's my professional services team, and every small business entrepreneur needs to make sure to start with professional service advisors, at least in the legal and accounting categories.

Having a team of professional service advisors ensures you'll get the best advice in order to make informed decisions for your business. Remember, you're only paying for their advice—you don't have to take it. On many occasions, I didn't take their advice, only to find out later I should have listened to them. For example, my CPA, George Stewart, advised me a few years ago to close some locations that weren't adding to the bottom line. He reminded me that I wasn't in the business of creating jobs for others, especially when I was struggling to keep my doors open in the first place. I didn't take his advice. Instead, I waited until the recession hit hard in 2008, and then I ended up closing a couple of locations he'd advised me to close years earlier. Wow, what a painful and expensive lesson that was.

Hindsight is 20/20 of course, and your advisors are there only to advise, not to nag you to death, or to make you do anything. You still have the freedom to choose and make your own decisions, even with professional advisors around you. Just keep in mind that you're paying them for their professional advice, not just opinions. Ask them to be truthful with you at all times, even to be hard on you, and to help you make the difficult decisions that will be needed from time to time.

I do want to add that in addition to George Stewart advising me to close down a couple of non-performing locations back in 2004 and 2005, my operations manager extraordinaire, Rosemary Bennetts, had given me the same advice years earlier. Sometimes the advice you need is sitting right in front of you, yet you don't heed it for whatever reason. In my case, I had to go through it and figure out how much pain I could bear before finally realizing that my non-performing locations were not going to perform better in the midst of the recession.

In addition to the professional services team, I added Rosemary Bennetts, who started out as the receptionist, transcriptionist, physical therapist aide, nighttime janitor—just about everything else we needed in order to get our business up and off the ground. We also added the young physical therapist my agent's daughter knew from physical therapy school in Southern California.

So there you have it, I had a team!

And before I knew it, we were celebrating our twentieth anniversary! That's a remarkable achievement, considering the fact that most small businesses (according to small business industry standards and statistics) won't survive past their second year.

Rosemary is still there and doing as remarkable a job as always. She's semi-retired now, and in her selfless way, has groomed a couple of physical therapists, Lisa Frahm, P.T. and Jodi Kuhn, P.T. to help manage the business.

Despite all the obstacles of running The Donaldson Clinic over the past twenty years (a partnership break-up, multiple locations, some wayward employees, non-performing locations, etc.), we've been a success, and we continue moving into the future, learning from the past and going forward as the great team we are.

With all that experience, I can offer a little advice about being a small business entrepreneur. So, how can *you*, as a small business entrepreneur, implement a successful strategy to ensure *you* will be around for decades to come? Ask yourself the following questions and find the answers to them.

- Have you surrounded yourself with the best team?

- Do you continue seeking advice, and learning and growing?

- Is it all about "you," or is it about your employees and your clientele?

- What is your outlook for the future?

- Are you positioned for the next set of opportunities that may come your way?

- Are you prepared for the next economic downturn?

- Are you open to "change," willing and able to "change" as you need to?

- What are you doing to market your business?

- What are you afraid of?

- Do you enjoy your work?

- What is your plan for five years from now? Ten years from now?

- What is your succession plan in case something happens to you?

- Are you able to make the "hard decisions" when it comes to downsizing your business or terminating employees?

- What organizations and groups do you belong to? Rotary? Chambers of Commerce? Business networking groups? Boards and committees? (The Chambers of Commerce in both Seattle and Tacoma were instrumental in helping me to develop my skills and grow as a businessperson.)

These questions are just a few of many to keep in front of you so you are able to answer them at all times as a business owner. It's not always going to be pretty, but you have to prepare yourself for every obstacle, challenge, and situation that may come your way. Many times, you may not even see the situation come in front of you, and it may just catch you unexpectedly. You have to think quickly on your feet and make swift decisions for the good of your team and your business.

Nothing gives me greater joy than to see small businesses succeed. I believe in buying locally and supporting small business entrepreneurs whenever I can. Small businesses have an uphill battle in every neighborhood, if only because they will rarely get to the price point the large corporations get, so they don't have a large margin. One reason why I admire small business entrepreneurs is that they have to be creative, intuitive, quick-thinking, offer much better customer service, and many times find employees right in their neighborhoods. Small business owners create jobs and hire from the community, and they make wonderful contributions in numerous ways to our communities. Consequently, I think everyone should respect and appreciate small businesses and the entrepreneurs who have the vision to create and sustain them.

I continue moving forward with my small business by being a good delegator and general manager as I work closely with other managers. A great adage I have heard is, "As a small business owner, you want to run your business, and not have your business run you." Doesn't that make sense? When you run your business effectively, you have more free time to promote your business in a variety of ways you just can't do from behind a desk between 8 a.m. and 5 p.m. That requires delegation and trust. You have to be able to delegate responsibilities and empower others to delegate, too. Then trust they will get the job done and hold them accountable.

My business didn't get to the size it is overnight. As I mentioned earlier, at first it was just me, Rosemary, and a physical therapist. The halls rang hollow many days/weeks/months due to a lack of patients and business. Many days, we wondered whether we were going to make it and whether we would fill the space we had rented.

Every small business entrepreneur has questions and doubts at first. You'll have restless and sleepless nights. I recall how during our annual meetings, my CPA Colin Brine would ask me, "James, as the business owner, what keeps you up at night?" That calls for some deep introspection and it's something that all small business owners need to ask themselves.

But when all is said and done, there's nothing better than to look at a business that's performing well, providing jobs, adding something to the bottom line, participating in community events, and establishing a sterling reputation along the way. There's nothing like it!

You can do the same thing. Help is abundant and resources are just about everywhere. Even in difficult economic times, opportunities are plenty. It takes a person with vision, energy, and the ability to make a 100 percent effort to take advantage of opportunities in order to be successful. All small businesses are operating on shoestring budgets in this day and age, but it can be done. Those that utilize the best talent and work together as a team will survive and thrive.

You'll go through many difficulties as a small business owner. Don't worry about it; it's par for the course!

In the twenty-plus years I've been a small business owner, I've come full circle. I started out with a business partner, but that ended after about seven years. We started with one location, which eventually grew to five locations, but now we're back to one location. At times, we added a lot to our bottom line, and other times, we went into debt. That's the life of a small business owner. Not many people understand what that's all about, except for other small business owners.

In the spring of 2009, I decided to close our Mukilteo location. I went to the Mill Creek office and met with Rosemary Bennetts. When I told her I'd decided to close the Mukilteo location, we both shed a few tears and then some sighs of relief as we released the stress we'd been under for the last several years as we tried to keep the business going. I told her how much I appreciated her supporting me as I explored and fulfilled some of my dreams of creating and establishing a physical therapy business in the heart of underprivileged and underserved neighborhoods. I knew it wasn't the best business model, but it was something I had really wanted to do, and Rosemary hung in there with me. You don't find that kind of support very often.

I told Rosemary that was the end of expanding the business to multiple locations, so she wouldn't have to worry about it again. She made me promise, and double promise (I'm not sure how much water that holds) that I would stick to my word and I intend to.

The Donaldson Clinic established itself as a physical therapy business that employs licensed physical therapists who have worked long and hard to achieve their various levels of expertise. We take great pride in surrounding our physical therapists with the support they need in order to provide outstanding services. Customer care and the success of our patients is our focus, and I am proud of the services we have been able to provide to help our many patients recover through our physical therapy services.

When I was recovering from my injury, the Dallas Mavericks had supplied a stretch limousine for me to travel to and from my physical therapy appointments, especially when I was in a full-length leg cast and unable to drive myself. From that concept, I established a courtesy shuttle van service to transport our patients from home or office to their physical therapy appointments and back again.

As the years went on, I developed a passion for the fitness business. So I decided to add a small fitness center alongside the physical therapy clinic. I had seen other clinics do the same throughout the country, and I knew it could work if we had synergy between the two ends of the business. Unfortunately, before we could get the fitness/physical therapy centers up and running, the economy took a nose dive and those models never had time to prove themselves. One of the joys of being a business entrepreneur is that you can be creative and implement different ideas into your business when the time is right and when they fit the model and market you're working within. Who knows what ideas I may yet implement in the future?

As a small business entrepreneur myself, I've appreciated the help I've received, and I have a deep passion for giving back by helping other small businesses. I'm the former vice chair of small business for both the Tacoma and the Greater Seattle Chambers of Commerce. In fact, I've become affectionately known as the "Big Man of Small Business." Now I am branching out into business consulting especially geared toward small business entrepreneurs. I conduct weekly phone conferences with several clients to help ensure they're doing the right thing and to encourage them along the way. If you want to be part of our conference calls and the exciting entrepreneurial adventures we're pursuing, contact me through my website at **www.StandingAboveTheCrowd.com** or email me at **JamesD@StandingAbovetheCrowd.com.**

I'd like to conclude this chapter with the key things to remember if you want to succeed as a small business owner.

THE SMALL BUSINESS ENTREPRENEUR'S TOP TEN PLAYBOOK

As a former professional athlete for nearly twenty years, I've been able to utilize skills and knowledge I learned from sports to help me to become a successful small business person.

Like a well-played game, all businesses will go through their natural cycles of ebbs and flows. You, as a small business entrepreneur, need to know when to call a timeout, change out your players, or when to run another play. Sports have taught me the value of team play, camaraderie, working toward common goals, learning from your temporary setbacks, and the ability to pick yourself up, dust yourself off, and keep on going.

If I were to put together a Top Ten list of "must haves," whether you're a startup company or a well-established business, it would go something like this:

1. Have a Vision

Where is it that you see your business in three to five years? How do you want it to look? How do you want it to run? Do you have a business plan? Do you have a Mission Statement? Do you have a Vision Statement? What is your succession plan?

2. Believe in Your Talent

Talent by itself is never enough. All too often, people with tremendous talent come up far too short from ever fulfilling their potential. You have to believe in your talent, be passionate about your talent, continue to invest in your talent, and surround yourself with the best talent available.

3. Assemble Your Team

A smart business entrepreneur makes sure that he or she is surrounded by talented professionals and not just a bunch of "yes" people. It's essential that you have a professional corporate attorney, CPA, financial advisor, bookkeeper, insurance person, and a front office manager as part of your team. An attorney and CPA are a must from the start, and you can add additional pieces to your team as you grow.

Be sure that you take the advice of your professional advisors; after all, that's what you pay them for. You may not always like what they have to say, but it's important to listen to them.

4. Empower Your Team

Equip your team members with the resources they need in order to be successful. In addition to helping them be successful, you'll be successful too. It's tempting to take shortcuts in order to save money, but it's important to keep your team up to speed in this day and age of high technology and development.

Your team will consist of professional advisors and everyday employment personnel. No matter what positions they occupy in your business, it's important they have the tools they need in order to help your business be the best it can be.

Another thing to keep in mind is to delegate responsibility and decision-making capabilities to various personnel throughout your company. An employee who feels empowered by the owner is a much more productive employee.

5. Peer Networking

One of the most valuable activities you can involve yourself in as a business owner is networking with your peers. Numerous opportunities exist for you to get outside of your business and network with other business owners.

Groups such as Chambers of Commerce, Rotary, Business Associations, and several weekly or monthly membership-based networking groups all can provide you with contacts and information to help your business grow. Make sure you attend one or two networking activities a month in order to promote your business and find out about other businesses in your community.

6. Realize Early on That You Don't Know Everything

Most business owners find themselves at various stages of their businesses, having to wear a multitude of hats. That's okay from time to time, but it's also important to keep in mind that other people are out there who can do a much better job than you in certain areas simply because they can bring a different perspective or more knowledge to the task. Every business owner will find him- or herself at the early stages of owning a business fulfilling just about every role imaginable, be it answering phones, scheduling clients, marketing, and/or keeping the books, and that's fine from time to time (as a matter of fact, it's good to learn every position in your business), but you don't want your business to rely on you having to fill every role.

As soon as you're able, delegate responsibilities to others on your team so they feel more valuable, and it eases the workload on you.

7. Realize Early on You Can't Do Everything

Similar to what's above, realizing early on that you can't do everything is a key to business success. There is a very high "burnout" factor for owners who have an "I can do it all by myself" attitude and refuse to delegate responsibilities to other members of the team. You may feel like no one can do it better than you (and that may be true), but if you want to keep your team engaged with a sense of ownership and empowerment, it's important to delegate responsibilities to them because it shows a sense of trust and confidence in the rest of your team.

Plenty of opportunities will arise for you as a business owner to "burn the midnight oil" so you might as well wait for those opportunities to roll around and be well rested and prepared when they do.

8. Stay Current

With technology advancing at warp speed, it's important for every business owner to stay up-to-date with some of the latest and greatest resources to help your business. It's true that there's so much out there that one cannot possibly absorb it all, but that goes back to the matter of you needing to be an owner who can keep his/her "head up" to see the big picture and opportunities in front of you and not get wrapped up in a "nose to the grindstone" mentality and approach.

Be adventuresome and daring in trying new techniques and technology that can help enhance your business. It's okay to take a "trial run" at various techniques just to see how they may fit into your business. One thing is certain, "Nothing stays the same, and change is the only constant." You've got to keep up with the ever-changing world we live in.

9. Don't Be Afraid of Change

Even if you feel you aren't changing, the world around you is. It's only natural for us to get complacent and to keep doing the same old thing because that's what we've always done. More importantly, if you aren't changing, you can bet that your competitors are, and most likely trying to change for a competitive advantage over you.

I've got a great quote on the wall in my office that says, "Change is inevitable…but growth is optional." I don't know about you, but I choose to grow.

One of the advantages of having a diverse team is that differences in people offer a broad range of perspectives and opinions. Older employees tend to stick to a tried-and-true method that may or may not be outdated, while younger employees have fresh brand-new ideas you may want to consider implementing if the time seems right.

10. Find Your MVP

In order for a small business to thrive, it's important for it to operate as a team. In order for a team to thrive, it will have many movable and variable parts that need to stay coordinated.

Every team has an MVP (Most Valuable Person) whom the owner feels comfortable and confident enough in to have that person as his/her "Go-To-Guy." For me that person is my operations manager, Rosemary Bennetts, who has been with me from day one for over twenty years.

Your MVP may or may not be the most visible or well-known person on the team. Your MVP may be someone who is tucked away in a back office, with his or her sleeves rolled up, and battling daily in the trenches in order to keep your business running. Your MVP may be your front desk person, or the hot shot salesperson you have out in the community. Whatever the case, work closely with your MVP (he or she will most likely know how the business works better than you do) and recognize and show appreciation for that person in an appropriate manner.

By following these top ten plays, you will have the basics required to be a successful small business entrepreneur.

Chapter 15

POLITICS
A GAME OF ANOTHER SORT

*Politicians are like diapers; they both need to be changed often and
for the same reason.*
— Mark Twain

The last thing I ever wanted to be was a "politician," but the reason I chose to run for a political office was so I could better serve the communities I truly care about.

Up until just a few years ago, if you asked me what I thought about politics, I would have told you, "I can't stand politics and I can't stand politicians." My close friends who know me well still remind me how often I talked like that.

Now, I realize that it wasn't so much that I really couldn't stand politics and politicians. It was more that politics seemed so frustrating and so futile at times because of the political process people implement and the political games they play. Try as we may to be nonpartisan, everything we do in life is partisan in nature. Even when we talk about being on a "team," doesn't that simply come down to "our team versus their team"? It doesn't get much more partisan than that.

So when you look at the political landscape and the very nature of it, it is going to be partisan. You're going to have the "haves versus the have-nots," the "conservatives versus the liberals," the "rich versus the poor," the "white-collar versus the blue-collar," and the "white, black, brown, yellow, and red people" fighting each other for their pieces of the rock. That's all partisan if you ask me.

So that's one of the big reasons I stayed away from politics in general. It seemed like no matter who was in charge, nothing really changed significantly. Serious issues still exist pertaining to race, prejudice, oppression, suppression, bigotry, hatred, unequal access and unequal opportunity, violation of civil rights, and the basic fulfillment of the American Dream on the part of so many people. I figured I should just stay out of that mess and instead do the best I could by trying to make the world a better place.

I wasn't oblivious to politics; I just picked and chose where I would and would not participate in the process. At times I wouldn't participate by voting because I didn't feel there was a candidate worthy of my vote. Many times, I would vote for whom I thought was the best candidate rather than along party lines. I feel that's the best way we can exercise our right to vote so we can ensure we are putting the best people in office in the first place, regardless of what party they represent; however, few politicians are unwilling to tow the party line, and I think that's why more and more of the populace are choosing the "Independent" classification. Independents are sort of like "free agents"—they can play the field and not be tied to one party or another. Voting for independents may actually not be a bad way to go because it will force candidates from the Republican and Democratic parties to work even harder for those swing votes.

As the saying goes, "if they could see me now," many of my friends from ten, twenty, and thirty years ago wouldn't recognize the person I've become through my involvement in the political landscape, not only in my hometown of Seattle, but across the whole state of Washington. I've come to realize that the best way truly to make a difference is to become involved in the political process. Not necessarily as a candidate for elected office, but at least involved in the voting process, volunteering time on the campaign for someone whom you truly support and feel will make a difference, and/or contributing financially to a campaign to assist your candidate in his or her efforts to be successful.

I found out quickly that politics is a game of another sort. There's a lot of strategy involved and a lot of "chalkboard sessions" that take place in the strategy "war rooms" or campaign offices that are set up during the campaign. It's a game where you definitely have to do your homework, be on top of the issues, have a thick skin, be ready for battle each and every day, work as a team, and fight to the bitter end for what you believe will be in the best overall interest of the constituents you represent. It can be "down and dirty" at times, with all the pettiness and name-calling, but as I did in my mayoral campaign in 2009 and as I emphasize throughout this book, you have to **Stand Above the Crowd** and not let all the little petty things bring you down.

You learn quickly who your friends are, and who will be there for you from start to finish, through thick and thin. I found out how quickly people will bail on you as soon as you take a dip in the polls or you plateau in terms of fundraising. In my campaign for the office of Mayor for the City of Seattle, I went through two campaign managers before I settled on my third one, Cindi Laws, who helped us fight tooth-and-nail to a respectable fourth-place finish (out of eight candidates, which included a two-term incumbent mayor who finished third and a multi-term city councilwoman who finished fifth).

All in all, I truly enjoyed the process, and in a sense, I felt that my years of preparation as a professional athlete, being competitive by nature, understanding the issues pertaining to the City of Seattle, and having a passion for giving back to my community, had me tailor-made to be a candidate. I feel that I would have been a very good Mayor for Seattle simply because of my abundance of common sense and fair play. My life transcends every ethnic, educational, and social boundary, and I've been very involved in the community for the thirty years I've lived in Seattle. I've rolled up my sleeves when it's been time to roll up my sleeves and worked in the trenches, and I've also put on a suit and tie to sit in the same room with all of the "who's who" around Seattle and the state of Washington.

Now that I have a taste for what the game of politics is all about, I have a passion to continue to be involved with it in one capacity or another. I'm not sure what that looks like at this point, but I do stay current with all of the political issues of the day as they pertain to Seattle and our great state of Washington.

MENTORS

I often get asked how I got involved with politics and what it takes to be successful at it. In 2007, I was having a lunch meeting with several community leaders in The Hilltop neighborhood of Tacoma, Washington. The Hilltop is notorious for gang activity, drug dealing, prostitution, homelessness, and aggressive panhandling...all occurring in broad daylight. It's been that way there for the last twenty or thirty years.

In 2001, I had established The Donaldson Clinic in The Hilltop. For me it was a way of giving back to the neighborhood, and I was passionate about making a difference there through a positive contribution. The clinic we established at that location was a smaller version of what we had started in the more established suburban area of Milk Creek, north of Seattle.

I felt a clinic in The Hilltop would be a wonderful way to provide professional services to a neighborhood that had been historically neglected and underutilized. For the eight years we were there, we provided excellent physical therapy services and a fitness center for the community. The clinic was never a "moneymaker" for us, but that was beside the point, and we were able to subsidize it to a great extent from our more established Mill Creek location. It wasn't the best business model to implement as I mentioned in the last chapter, but my personal passion for community involvement had made me go down that road anyway.

During my lunch meeting in 2007, I was surrounded by several of my wonderful mentors, namely, Brian Ebersole, Drew Ebersole, Felix Flannigan, and my dear friend, Tim Johnson. Running around together was a hoot for all of us, and we always had a great time together.

Brian Ebersole had been an established elected official/politician for about thirty-five years. He had served as Mayor of Tacoma, City Councilman, majority and minority whip in the state capital in Olympia, and several other positions throughout his long, distinguished career. Now, in semi-retirement mode, Brian goes around the state of Washington identifying potentially electable Democratic candidates. Brian is a ball of energy and one of the most optimistic and entertaining guys I know.

Over lunch, Brian kept playfully poking at me and saying, "James, you have to run for office, you have to run for office." He told me to take a look at all the things I'd been doing over the last twenty or thirty years in the community—mentoring, tutoring, running a small business, athletics, and being a positive role model. He said that all those things added up to a very electable candidate for office. Plus, I had a sterling reputation, and I had never been in trouble. Brian was so excited over lunch that he just wasn't going to let go of the idea. I remember telling him over lunch, "Brian, go away. I can't stand politics and politicians." But Brian had me promise him one thing: that I would pay attention (for literally the first time in my life) to the political process in the primaries that were coming up that August in Seattle. He encouraged me to find a couple of candidates I liked and to follow them on the campaign trail. He said, "After that, come back to me and we'll have a discussion about it."

Well, I took his advice. I followed around a couple of Seattle City Council candidates during the primaries. It didn't take me long to find the whole process exciting and even exhilarating. I remember coming back to my home after attending a couple of candidate forums saying to myself, "They're talking about a lot of the same issues that we work on with some of the various boards and committees I belong to." I thought to myself, *I can do that*, and what better way, I figured, was there for me to serve my community than from City Hall?

So that's how I actually got started in the whole political process. I give all the credit to Brian Ebersole for getting me started, and for coaching and mentoring me along the way. It's not that Brian and I are carbon copies of each other; that's pretty far from ever being the case, but I was able to take a lot of his experience and apply it to what I would experience on the political campaign trail. Brian has such a "rah rah" approach that he became my coach and my cheerleader at the same time, and he was there from start to finish. On many occasions, he made the forty-five minute drive from Tacoma to Seattle to sit in on several "strategy meetings" and campaign events that we were having during the course of my campaign.

RUNNING FOR OFFICE

Not many people remember, but when I first started out on the campaign trail, I was a candidate for the office of City Councilman. After getting up to speed on quite a few of the issues in several meetings with Brian Ebersole and a few key people around Seattle, I made my announcement to run in the spring of 2008. It was an exciting time for me because I was embarking upon a whole new endeavor that, up until a few years before, I had never envisioned myself doing. How many times has that happened to you where you find yourself taking on a whole new endeavor or challenge that you never thought possible? How did you handle it? What did you do to prepare for it? What type of team and people did you surround yourself with?

As I mentioned before, you find out quickly who your friends are and who will bail on you as soon as times start getting tough. The beginning of my campaign went relatively smoothly, and I was able to generate quite a bit of "buzz" because of the "celebrity nature" I brought to the campaign. We used that buzz to our advantage by booking radio spots and doing as many interviews as possible.

Besides the buzz we were able to generate for my candidacy, word went out throughout my network of friends and associates that I was running for office. It was hilarious in a lot of instances because so many of my friends just couldn't believe that I, after all these years of detesting politics, was running for political office. I reassured everyone that I was serious and just as passionate about running for political office as anything else I'd ever done in my life, including being a professional athlete, a small business entrepreneur, and involved in community affairs.

Running for office requires a big sacrifice of time, energy, family life, relationships, friends and associates, money, and just about everything else in your daily routine. It can be done though if you have a good strategy in place and work together as a team. I didn't waste any time implementing my "Total Team Concept," and even though some people laughed at the mindset I was bringing into the political landscape, for me it was the best way to go, and it also made everyone else I was representing feel as if he or she were part of the process.

I recall a meeting I had with one of the incumbent Seattle City Council members where I mentioned to him that I was looking forward to joining the Council and being part of the team. He laughed at me in a belittling kind of way and said, "We're not a team. We're individual political entities representing our constituents." *Wow*, I thought to myself, *that's too bad because the only way you can really get things done is by working together.* He assured me that when it comes time to try to move things forward, you do so by getting a consensus (or at least a majority vote) among the other Council members, but there's always a trade-off of your political cachet that you're able to build up along the way. That aspect of politics everyone has to deal with, and "It is what it is." Basically, you scratch my back and I'll scratch yours. So knowing all that, I was bound and determined to be the best team member I could be among a bunch of individual entities, and my style would be that I would bridge the gap and work both sides of the aisle as smoothly and efficiently as I possibly could, without compromising myself.

On one occasion while I was following a candidate on the campaign trail, I challenged one of the incumbents who was saying one thing but then voting just the opposite. It was an issue pertaining to paper versus plastic bags of all things, and the council member at first gave this long, rambling speech on the merits of plastic bags, only to vote against it when it came up for a vote. When I asked the council person about it, he told me he was going to need "political capital" in the hallways of City Hall in the future, so he had learned to show support and vote in favor of some things he was against (for the public record) in exchange to gain support on issues he wanted to get passed and where he would need votes to push them through. I told him that was not leadership…that was "politics as usual"! I know there's a certain amount of give-and-take in everything, but I want to try my best to stand up for—and vote for—what I believe in.

One of the first sacrifices I made along the way on my campaign trail concerned my girlfriend. She and I had been dating for a couple of years, but she ran for the hills as soon as she heard I was going into politics. Until then, I didn't know she was so against politics. She explained to me that when she was a little girl, an uncle of hers had been a prominent politician who brought great shame upon the family with some scandalous misdoings. Apparently, that event had influenced her so much that she had told herself she would never, ever date a politician. I tried to reason with her and let her know that I was not "a politician *per se*"—I was the same old guy she had known for the past couple of years—but she wouldn't listen and put an end to our relationship.

What could I do? What could I say? The political bug had bitten me pretty deeply, and the passion I had for running for elected office was consuming my every waking moment. I told her that running for office was what I really wanted to do with my life, and that I was moving forward with it, with or without her. Now that I look back on it, that sounded pretty cold, but I really felt a "calling" of sorts to pursue my political ambitions.

So I started out on my campaign trail feeling somewhat lonely, and word spread pretty quickly that I had broken up with my girlfriend and was a single man again. Soon after, I was invited to a big political dinner by a prominent community leader who insisted I sit at her table. When she asked whether I needed one or two tickets, I said I only needed one, but then I muttered something about how I wished I needed two, but my girlfriend had just broken up with me. She told me not to worry; she had just the woman for me. I didn't know what she meant, but I trusted that she knew what she was doing, so I attended the event by myself, only to find the seat next to me empty.

Within a few minutes, lo and behold, one of the most beautiful ladies I had ever laid eyes on sauntered up to sit down in the seat right next to me. My "matchmaker" friend, sitting across the table from me, winked as if to say, *She's for you.* I thought my prayers had been answered! I was in a terrible emotional state because I was no longer with my girlfriend, and I was praying and praying that God would either bring us back together again, or provide someone new for me with whom I could have a great relationship.

God works in mysterious ways! It wasn't long before this beautiful young lady and I were an item and began a great relationship. I was filled with excitement and enthusiasm not only for my burgeoning political career, but also for an exciting new relationship filled with promise. My new young lady friend wasn't just beautiful; she was also very involved in politics and knew just about everyone from Olympia to Seattle in the political field. I envisioned the two of us becoming the next prominent couple on the political scene. That was exciting, and it was wonderful while it lasted.

Unfortunately, the relationship didn't last all that long. It was only three or four months before things started falling apart. It was pretty apparent that even though we were both very involved in politics, and we looked like a wonderful couple, we had political and value differences we just weren't able (or willing) to overcome. I won't go into all the nitty-gritty details at this point; I'll just say it was great while it lasted, and we really did have a love for each other that was truly wonderful.

Long story short, my girlfriend who had run for the hills at the start of my political career reemerged on the scene and into my life after about ten months, and we began talking again and decided to resume our relationship where we left off. She ended up being a vital part of the campaign when I was a mayoral candidate, especially in the areas of support and caring for me no matter what the outcome of the campaign was going to be.

It took a while for people to realize I was more than just another "jock" or celebrity seeking political office for whatever attention, fame, or fortune it might offer (Let me tell you; it offers very little of either!). Because of my quiet demeanor and gentlemanly ways, a lot of people didn't feel I was up to the task of being a "politician." Since a lot of people didn't know me personally, they didn't know how tough I was going to be or whether I would be able to deal with the "down and dirty" of politics.

When I met with one of the foremost political consultants in town, she really had her doubts about whether I would be tough enough for the game of politics...until after we met. When I arrived at her office for a meeting, she looked me up and down and then told me she had doubted whether I was tough enough for politics because she had heard I was such a nice guy. Then she said, "I've been watching some of your game tapes, and you're a tough guy all right; you can handle yourself." Then she proceeded to ask me several questions to see whether I would become rattled.

In a rapid-fire style, she asked:

- Why are you single?

- Have you ever been married?

- Do you have a girlfriend?

- Do you do drugs?

- Have you ever been busted?

After several such questions, she gave me the rundown and the once-over and said, "Hmm, handsome, tall, good-looking, athletic, single, never been married, no kids...are you gay?"

I found myself stammering and stuttering over that one as I managed to mumble a few words. "No, I'm not gay; of course I'm not gay. What makes you think something like that?"

As I answered each and every one of her questions, particularly the last one, she said, "Good, and if you're lying to me, it will come out sooner or later."

Once she was assured that I was telling her the truth on each and every one of her questions, she said, "Well, since you aren't married, and you aren't gay, here's something that may be helpful strategic-wise for you, and that is to be seen with an assortment of beautiful women around town at various high-profile places. That will put to rest any rumor that you might be gay. People will look upon you as a nice-looking single guy who's never been married, is over fifty, with no children, so the rumor that you might be gay will persist and dog you every step of the way, so being seen with women is a good way to snuff it out." See what I mean about politics being very strategic?

As I continued running for the City Council seat, I started to feel I was getting the hang of it pretty quickly. I was up to speed on all the issues, and even though it was a very tough fundraising climate due to the economic recession that hit us in 2008, I didn't mind "dialing for dollars" and calling virtually everyone I knew for support. I also thought I handled myself pretty well when answering questions pertaining to the issues in our city. I did a lot of interviews for radio and newspapers and felt I was starting to emerge in the public's eye as more than just a jock—as someone who was actually a viable candidate for elected office.

Originally, when my mentor Brian Ebersole planted the seed in me to run for political office, he encouraged me to run for the office of Mayor of Seattle, or a legislative position such as State Representative or Senator, or even the U.S. Congress. That's Brian Ebersole's sometimes over-optimistic style. He shoots for the moon in just about everything he does. I told him that was way beyond anything I could imagine at that point, especially with my being a "political newbie" and not having any political experience under my belt. I didn't let his suggestion just go in one ear and out the other though, and I always held onto the possibility of running for either Seattle City Council or Mayor.

Meanwhile, growing anxiety in Seattle city politics spread about who was going to run against our increasingly unpopular incumbent mayor? Mayor Greg Nickels had established a pretty powerful administration that was in some ways effective, but in many other ways very intimidating and isolating to the general public and to the Seattle City Council members. Actually, because of Mayor Nickels' perceived style, relationships weren't too good between the City of Seattle and the state capital of Olympia. So something had to be done.

I would say that about 90 percent of my many meetings at that time wouldn't wrap up until a discussion had taken place about who was going to run against our incumbent mayor. The business community felt it needed better representation. Olympia was hoping for a better relationship with Seattle. Communities and neighborhoods around Seattle were screaming to be heard by the Mayor's Office, and feeling very neglected and isolated. So the question kept being asked on the campaign trail, "Who's going to run against Greg Nickels?"

I started to flash back to some of my conversations with Brian Ebersole and recalled his encouraging me to run for the office of mayor. As with anything in life, once you start envisioning something, and then you start imagining it as reality—what it could actually be—it starts coming to life, and it starts gnawing at you until you do something about it.

Have you ever had anything like that happen to you? Where you feel something you've been either purposely avoiding or something that someone has been encouraging you to take a look at starts coming closer and closer to reality until you feel you can actually tackle it and be successful. That's how I came about my decision to run for the office of mayor.

When you start envisioning things as reality, they become possible. And then when they become possible, as soon as you start putting some effort into them, they become doable. Once something becomes doable, you start tasting your first bit of success at it; then it's something you won't let go of until you're actually successful at it and you've given every bit of effort toward it that you can. That's how successful people become successful. They don't run from a vision, reality, or something that's doable, and by not running but instead pursuing, they are led to success. They go head-on into it and tackle it with all the gusto they can.

My pastor emeritus, Samuel B. McKinney, has told a story many times to our church that beautifully illustrates this point. It's the story of a majestic bald eagle encountering an oncoming storm. This magnificent bird, with a ten-foot wingspan and armed with a vicious beak and razor-sharp talons, is flying along when he spots an oncoming storm on the horizon. The storm is moving toward him at a pretty rapid clip, and before the eagle can decide whether to fly around the storm (the storm is so huge there's no way he can fly around it), fly over it (the storm is so immense that no bird can fly at that altitude), or to turn tail and try to outrace the storm (an impossibility because the storm is moving at such a rapid pace), the eagle decides that his best option is to face adversity head-on. So the eagle starts flapping rapidly to pick up speed and flies right into the heart of the storm only to find himself tossed around, beaten and battered, and not sure which way is up, before he is spat out on the other side. As the eagle gets his bearings, he realizes first and foremost that he is still alive, and he begins to flap his wings again and regains his composure and his ability to continue flying. He is beaten and battered, and he ends up missing quite a few feathers, but the fact is, he faced adversity and emerged on the other side all the better for the adversity (minus a few feathers) and the experience he went through.

Reverend McKinney reminds us that there are three stages of life in which we constantly find ourselves. One is relative tranquility and peace (the calm before the storm), the second is finding ourselves in the midst of the storm, and the third is exiting from the storm, only to find another storm in the not-too-far-off distance that we have to encounter again. Only, we're better able to face that next storm because of the one we just endured and overcame.

Sometimes that's how we have to face adversity. We have to realize that it's better to face it head on than try to sidestep it, go under or over it, or turn and run from it.

So, the opportunity for me to run for mayor lay right in front of me. At that time, early 2009, no one else had yet announced an intention to run for that office. I continued to say to myself, "I can't rightfully stand by and watch our very unpopular two-term incumbent mayor waltz right back into his third term, totally uncontested." I would constantly say to myself, "If not me, who? If not now, when?" So in early 2009, I made my decision to run for mayor.

As soon as I made my decision, the political consultants I was working with jumped ship and ran for the hills because they feared the wrath of our powerful incumbent mayor. I understood where they were coming from; they had political careers on the line, but I didn't.

I also overestimated the support I would get from the business (especially small business) community. I found out quickly that many times the business community is going to support the incumbent even if it doesn't fully embrace how things have been going. It's the old adage of, "the devil they know versus the devil they don't." (I don't consider myself a devil by any means, by the way.)

Those things happen, and they are part of the political process. I soon found another political consultant to work with, but when he saw that we weren't making as much progress as he had hoped, he jumped ship also and joined the campaign of a long-term city councilwoman who had announced she was running for mayor. You learn quickly who you want in your foxhole and who you don't.

I was lucky to have a young woman named Cindi Laws step in to rescue my campaign. Cindi has made a career out of taking on campaigns and candidates who are long shots to win and going against the odds. She really gets her juices flowing when she can manage a woman or minority candidate. That's her passion!

Cindi stepped in and picked up the pieces from my campaign and managed to help us get a fourth-place finish among the eight candidates. She and I worked very well together, and as I told her several times during the campaign, "You're the coach; I'm the player. You draw up the play, and I run the ball." Again, my athletic background helped me go through a coaching change and keep working toward my goal.

For what it's worth, I felt we made a very respectable showing in the election. I thought I did a really good job on the campaign trail and in all the different debate forums and community meetings we attended. I was really hoping at least to make it out of the primaries, but it became pretty evident the night of the primaries that it wasn't to be. So I ended up coming in fourth place with about 9 percent of the vote and over 12,000 voters. Not bad for a "newbie," but for someone as competitive as I am, not good enough.

If nothing else, that experience definitely set the stage for whatever I may decide to do in the future in politics. I do have a keen interest in keeping my political efforts local, but you never know. I really enjoy the whole state of Washington, and although I live on the western end, my alma mater, Washington State University, is on the state's eastern side so I have a lot of love for all of Washington.

At this point, I mainly stay involved with the political issues of the day through the Greater Seattle Chamber of Commerce public affairs/policy council committee and several neighborhood community groups and committees around town. I enjoy attending meetings with various elected officials as they brief us on issues they're working on and/or challenges they may be having. I believe one of the keys to success is getting involved—and staying involved. It's also important to network with the appropriate people, groups and committees, and to make the most of those relationships.

ENCOURAGING OTHERS

If we prepare well, we have all the tools and resources we'll ever need to be successful at what we attempt. So we shouldn't fear failure, especially if we try. I never knew how well I would do as a political candidate until

I tried. Now that I have the hang of it, I feel that if I give it a try again I'll be successful. If nothing else, it's a great feeling to know you've tried something and have given it your best effort. Even to this day, people praise me for running for an elected office. Most people have no idea that they can do the same.

As I closed the doors on two of my favorite business locations and two of my favorite neighborhoods, The Hilltop in Tacoma and the Central Area of Seattle in 2007-8, I remember literally looking back over my shoulder as I walked away from both and saying to myself that the best way I could serve those neighborhoods was from City Hall in Seattle. At City Hall, I could be involved with policymaking, implementing needed changes, and directing resources toward those neighborhoods that could really utilize them. I could figure out ways to encourage businesses to invest in underserved neighborhoods. At City Hall, working with the other policymakers, we could work to come up with incentives to employ people who lived in those neighborhoods and put them back to work. We could work on keeping the neighborhoods clean, safe, graffiti-free, and ensure that our police officers were considered, not as enemies, but friends in the neighborhood.

That's my encouragement to others: Get involved with the political process and help make those changes for every community. It's one thing to be a shop owner and open up a storefront and hire people who live in the neighborhood. It's another to be an instrument of change that raises the overall tide so everyone benefits.

Get involved with the political process by every means possible. Be a voter, volunteer for political campaigns, and contribute to your favorite candidates so you can ensure the best people will represent you well.

I know there is an overwhelming sense of disenfranchisement and dis-connection among people in regards to the political process, especially with communities of color, but I'm here to say that the very best way a difference can be made and felt is through the political process. It's something we tend not to become too involved with, because like myself at an earlier stage in my life, there's a sense that no matter what we do it won't make a difference.

Now that I've had a chance to "look under the hood" of how the political process works and how it can benefit communities, I can see for myself that participating in that process is truly one of the best things a person can do.

Chapter 16

MAKE AN AGREEMENT WITH YOURSELF

Throughout my life, whether as a professional athlete, a business owner, or a politician, I have come to realize that if we are not true to ourselves, we will get pulled back and forth without a stable support system by the various people and events we encounter. So as we come to the last couple of chapters in this book, I want to emphasize the importance of being true to yourself, and the best way you can do that is to make promises or agreements to yourself that you do not break.

One of the best books I've read in recent memory is *The Four Agreements* by Juan Miguel Ruiz. It gives a great overview of how we're conditioned as young people, and then we spend the rest of our lives trying to deal with these "conditional" relationships we've formed with significant people (parents, siblings, teachers, and the like) in which we continue to grow further and further from who we "really are" in an ever-increasingly frustrating attempt to please them and fulfill whatever sense of attachment, appreciation, and love we seek. Ruiz explains, by contrast, that we really only need to make four agreements with ourselves and others. Below are the main points Ruiz makes, but I encourage you to read all of *The Four Agreements* for further understanding about making agreements with ourselves and others.

THE FOUR AGREEMENTS

Be Impeccable With Your Word

Be Impeccable With Your Word. Speak with integrity. Say only what you mean. Avoid using the word to speak against yourself or to gossip about others. Use the power of your word in the direction of truth and love.

Don't Take Anything Personally

Nothing others do is because of you, or at least rarely is any of it directly because of you. What others say and do is a projection of their own reality, their own dreams. When you are immune to the opinions and actions of others, you won't be the victim of needless suffering.

Don't Make Assumptions

Find the courage to ask questions and to express what you really want. Communicate with others as clearly as you can to avoid misunderstandings, sadness, and drama. With just this one agreement, you can completely transform your life.

Always Do Your Best

Your best is going to change from moment to moment; it will be different when you are tired as opposed to well-rested. Under any circumstances, simply do your best, and you will avoid self-judgment, self-abuse, and regret.

As Juan Miguel Ruiz points out, the agreements we make for ourselves, as opposed to the conditioned agreements we make with others, are in the long run much more beneficial to our overall well-being. The conditioned agreements we have in place, with many of the important and influential people in our lives, tend to prevent us from realizing our full potential because we fear losing relationships we have had for years, no matter how dysfunctional or conditioned they may have become.

How many times do we catch ourselves wondering what so-and-so would say or think if we chose to take a particular action, or even if they knew what we were thinking? Like most kids, we grow up to be the perfect little child our parents want us to be—at least while we're in our parents' presence, that's how we will appear. There's a constant tug-of-war when we are kids over who our parents want us to be; how they want us to think, speak, and act; what kinds of grades they expect us to bring home from school; and what they want us to grow up to be when we become adults, and our own inner sense of who we feel we really are and what we really want to accomplish with our lives. When we start pushing toward being authentic and true to our own natures, we start hearing that little inner voice that says, "Mama wouldn't be happy about that if she knew what you were doing," or "You know Daddy wouldn't approve of that," or "Little boys and little girls don't do those kinds of things."

That's how it is for all of us growing up; we're dealing with a constant tug-of-war that plays out inside of us. And then as we get a little older, usually during our teenage years, we really start testing the boundaries our parents set for us; we test them to see how much more we can get away with while still being the good little boys and girls who are forever pleasing in our parents' eyes. This point is where a lot of young people start going sideways. Such testing is natural for young people who want to experience the world around them. For myself, I used to take my bicycle off road and down by the banks of the Sacramento River to go up and down the sand dunes and levies on the bike trails there. Back then, kids were free to run around and explore the outdoors without fearing every stranger that came by. I remember how we used to jump onto the trains as they went by on their way down the tracks just to see where they would take us, only to find ourselves having to hoof it an extra long way home. Kids have always been adventurous and wanting to test the limits. Sometimes, I went down to the river with my parents' knowledge, but more often than not, I did it without them knowing. When I think back on it now, I realize how potentially dangerous it was, but back then, I was just being a kid.

There's a great saying that goes: "Be yourself because everyone else is already taken." If we take that advice to heart, then why do we spend so much time being everyone except who we really are? We know deep inside us who we are. We all should continue to move toward our true selves, with no disrespect toward others, especially toward those who mean so much to us.

How do we learn to be ourselves when we crave the love and acceptance of parents, relatives, and peers? We do it by being honest with ourselves and communicating effectively with others. If we take the time to learn and implement effective communication strategies, then we will be able to communicate with those who matter most and let them know that we appreciate their love, affection, acceptance, gifts, and the support they've showered upon us over the years, but we can also ask them, please, to take the time to listen to whom we are, where we want to go, and what we'd like to do with our lives; we can then let them know we would appreciate their continued love and support as we go through this process of defining and becoming who we are and whom we truly want to be. If need be, we can remind them that if they truly love us, they will let us live our own lives. Keep in mind that this move toward freedom and individuality will only work best once you are of legal age and no longer dependant on your parents; if you are under eighteen and reading this book, please continue doing what your parents say, but try communicating with them effectively, so you can start to create a win-win relationship instead of the dysfunctional, conditional relationship that is so common for most people and usually only holds them back from being everything they wish to be and can be in their lives.

By taking Juan Miguel Ruiz's advice to live by the Four Agreements, we can better deal with the conditional (and sometimes dysfunctional) relationships that have been formed throughout our lives. Those conditional relationships are formed first with our parents, then with our friends and our peers, then with our relationship partners as we get older, and then, guess what? The cycle repeats all over again with our own children as we form those conditional relationships with them. But once we set boundaries by using the Four Agreements, we can break that cycle and move forward in supportive and loving relationships with each other; those types of relationships will then help us to progress toward our goals and experience what we want in life.

As a person who practices and believes in the Christian faith, I understand that the only unconditional relationship and love a person will ever experience is God's love toward us. His love toward us is never changing, and it is always present even when we don't feel like He's alongside us. All you have to do is think back to the famous poem "Footprints in the Sand" to realize He's always there with us and supporting us even when we feel like we're all alone.

Once in a while, we'll come across people who will tell us they will love us forever, no matter what, and that their love is unconditional. I know that sounds good and feels good, and the person may truly mean it, but everyone has a breaking point where he or she will say, "No more. I can't go on loving this person under these conditions!" Therefore, when certain conditions arise, although they vary for each person, the love is either withdrawn or seriously altered. A lot of us feel that our dogs or cats are the epitome of loyalty, but even they will only take so much abuse before finally moving on to the neighbor's house down the street to find a loving home again.

At an early age, I developed a strong sense of independence and I understood that in order for me to make something of myself, I would have to teach and train myself not to fall prey to peer pressure or to negative influences. I give a lot of credit for that to my dad because he is a very disciplined and structured individual who seems to stand strong in the face of every kind of adversity. I grew up as most other kids grew up, rough-and-tumble, and testing the boundaries every now and then, but I still had that sense of respect for myself and for my parents.

I'd like to spend the rest of this chapter illustrating what the Four Agreements, as described in Juan Miguel Ruiz's book, mean to me and how I believe that by our making these four agreements with ourselves and taking them to heart, we will experience enormous benefits.

BE IMPECCABLE WITH YOUR WORD

Being impeccable with your word means, being truthful in everything you say; that includes the words you speak to others, but more importantly the words that inner voice in your head says to and about you. We all like to look in the mirror and talk about how flawlessly beautiful we are, but in reality, we know we're just saying that to make ourselves feel better. There's nothing wrong with giving ourselves a boost of self-esteem, but when we tell ourselves things that really aren't untrue, whether or not we realize they aren't true, that's where the problems begin.

Many times we tell ourselves things we know are not true so we can hide from the truth or escape blame and responsibility. Once we can squarely look ourselves in the mirror and be absolutely truthful with whatever situation we're going through and the role we are playing in it, it has a way of setting us free. As the old adage says, "The truth will set you free." Sadly, many times we are more in line with Jack Nicholson's famous line from *A Few Good Men*, "You can't handle the truth." How many of us can handle the truth?

Here's a little exercise I'd like for you to do. Take a serious assessment of who you are and where you are in life. Be real with yourself in a loving, constructively critical kind of way where you really break down all the various layers you tend to wrap around yourself, and get down to your true inner core. Ask yourself the hard questions, such as:

- Is it really so-and-so's fault that I didn't finish high school?

- Where do I place the blame for my last relationship not working out so well?

- Why am I holding a grudge against someone who has been long gone out of my life?

- How can I get back to feeling better about my weight and my size?

- What are the steps I can do to mend a broken relationship, or a broken heart?

As you can see, the questions could go on and on and on and would depend on your particular situation. They're going to be hard questions, and some of them might have frightening answers, but be brave and try to answer them anyway. If you can truthfully answer these kinds of questions and dig down deep into your inner core in the presence of just "me, myself, and I," you'll be amazed by the freedom you will realize. It's a tremendous sense of liberation once you start realizing the roles you have played in every situation you find yourself in over the course of your life. Truly understanding those roles and making sure you do better with them in the future will only make your life happier and easier. That happiness and sense of well-being, however, can only be achieved by being absolutely truthful with ourselves.

Being impeccable with our word when speaking to others means that "our word is gold." We are all human, and I realize we are all going to tell "little white lies," primarily in an attempt to spare someone's feelings from being hurt. That's a compassionate side that we all have, and such kindness is a beautiful thing. But we all need to use good judgment so that little white lie doesn't start growing into misshaped perceptions and a distorted sense of reality.

If you're integral with your word, others will come to trust in you because of your honesty and consistency. Our world is built on trust. When the trust level is high between others and ourselves, we all tend to get along so much better. It's when that sense of trust is betrayed that everything seems to come crashing down around us. Trust is a delicate thing, so we have to be careful how we communicate with each other, and we need to realize that the trust we have with each other is a very valuable thing.

If you find yourself in a situation where you have to (in actuality you choose to) tell an outright lie, or where an accumulation of little white lies have built up to a point that perception and reality are starting to go haywire, stop yourself and own up to it as soon as you can. Find a moment to pull aside the person with whom you're not being totally truthful and try to straighten things out as clearly as you can. Accept responsibility, and let that person know you didn't mean not to tell him or her the truth; say that you're sorry for not being completely honest and that you hope the other person can maintain his trust and confidence in you. By being upfront and stopping the lie from going any farther, you can keep the level of trust high, and even if it does dip down a little bit, it's just a temporary dip and not a destructive crash that ends the relationship. It's up to us to act quickly to mend the damage being done before it gets out of control.

Not being impeccable with your word is like the ocean constantly eroding away the beach and the coastline. It may not look like a lot of damage or changes are happening, but over time, you can definitely see that things have changed.

In most scenarios, we don't intentionally set out to hurt one another (especially without some good reason to do so). Once budding relationships are formed, they will grow into trust when people use integrity with their words. It's up to us to keep our words filled with that integrity.

DON'T TAKE ANYTHING PERSONALLY

Of the Four Agreements, not taking things personally is probably the most difficult for us. We all have a tendency to jump to assumptions, often just because we don't want to take the time to find out the facts we really need to know to fill in the blanks. When it comes down to not taking things personally, it's a whole other ballgame because our feelings are on the line and we are emotionally attached to others.

Deep down inside, we all want other people to like us, so it's easy for us to get our feelings hurt when they don't or when the trust we have instilled in another is betrayed one way or another.

You know what? If we just take the time to see the big picture, it makes it so much easier to see that in most cases events or things we may dislike were not even done with us in mind so there's no reason to take them personally. Without going too deep into the psychology for why we do take things personally, many times it is because we have an inner need or void that needs to be filled by the attachment and the conditioned relationship we have with those who are important to us.

Have you noticed how easy it is to have our feelings hurt by those who are closest to us? I once had a friend of mine tell me that "people can irk you...but friends and family can hurt you." That's so true because of the importance and trust we put on friends and family. We all experience the occasional flare-ups of people we work with, or that occasional bout of road rage toward complete strangers. That's nothing compared to how we really get our feelings hurt when those closest to us betray our trust in them from time to time.

I learned a long time ago, even before reading *The Four Agreements*, not to take anything personally. I developed an uncanny knack for taking a step back from a situation (at least psychologically) and seeing the bigger picture. I quickly learned the best way to deal with a problematic situation was not to take it personally. When I'm in a difficult situation, the first question I ask myself is: What role have I played in this? If I have direct involvement in the situation and have purposefully set out to hurt someone or to gain from the situation, then that's on me. If it turns out that the person in the situation I'm dealing with was trying to gain something from me and ended up coming away from it with less than he or she expected, and that person ends up getting upset with me, I realize quickly that it's not me the person is upset with, but the situation.

I can recall several friendships I've had over the years that ended up getting derailed and someone's feelings got hurt. When those situations occur, I try to play back the details of the friendship in my mind to see what role I played in the derailment. I ask myself:

- Was I deceitful?

- Was I trying to hurt that person?

- Was I trying to gain from our friendship?

- Did I betray the person's confidence and trust in me?

- Did I disrespect the person?

- Did I lie to him or her?

Questions like these really help me to get to the root cause of what happened to the friendship. I'm not afraid to take responsibility and own up to my share of the burden, and I keep in mind that "It takes two to tango" so we both have a role to play in the friendship. Just by keeping that concept in mind and asking myself those hard pointed questions, I can realize that the derailment of a friendship is not to be taken personally (I say "derailment" instead of "breakup" because unless someone really, really set out to hurt the other, my friendships and relationships tend only to become derailed; I then try with the other person's help to put the relationship back on track). By keeping these things in mind and following this process, I give myself and the other person involved the chance to make amends if we both so choose.

I've even learned not to take things personally in romantic relationships that didn't quite end up where the two of us may have intended. When relationships reach a romantic level, we really wear our personal feelings on our sleeves. I've had several girlfriends over the years quit speaking to me because they took the breakup of our relationship way too personally. Believe me, I know that emotions run differently in women compared to men, so I factor that in, and I know that sometimes things really do become personal. But what I try to do at the end of a romantic relationship is again to ask myself some hard questions about the role I played and what blame or responsibility I had in the relationship; that helps me not to take things personally no matter how emotional I may be feeling at the time. Rather than taking things personally, I try to look at the ended relationship as a learning experience and a clarification for the future of what I do want in my relationships.

For professional athletes, relationships can become especially difficult with family members who suddenly think because you've become successful that you are now their "golden goose" who will fulfill all their financial needs. While it's great to do whatever you can for your family, there are limits, and letting people know you can't support or help them as they wish can be difficult. They may see such behavior from you as a personal affront, when most of the time it shouldn't be taken personally, but it is really just business or common sense, or they have more grandiose notions of your success than you can live up to. It's hard to deal with these situations since you may risk ostracizing your family, but again, your family members need to learn not to take it personally, and you also need to realize that just because they set expectations on you does not mean you are responsible for taking care of them; you should not take their "issues" personally either.

I'm not saying it's easy not to take things personally, but if you keep this agreement with yourself at the front of your mind, you can at least tend to see the bigger picture and quickly realize any dynamics at play. You'll also feel a lot less stress and tension than if you let your emotions get out of control over something that wasn't personal to begin with.

DON'T MAKE ASSUMPTIONS

Making assumptions is probably one of the easiest things for us to do on a regular basis. Some assumptions are made naturally in the course of the day just for our basic human survival needs. For example, we assume the sun is going to come up in the morning and set in the evening. We make assumptions based on the fact that certain seasons of the year will yield predictable temperature ranges; we assume plants will bud in the spring, the days will be longest in the summer, the leaves will turn color in the fall, and we will have cold weather and snow in the winter. After eons and eons of that being the case, we can safely assume (global climate changes not withstanding) that such events will be the case throughout our lifetimes.

When it comes to human relationships, however, instead of making assumptions, we need to get our facts together. It's easy to make assumptions like "That must be what so-and-so is thinking," or to take a quick glance at a situation and assume we know all there is to know about it. We have to be careful about that because many times an assumption will take us down the wrong road where we will end up miles away from where we need to be in order to connect the dots.

As I watch the world around me operate at warp speed, I can only imagine that we will begin to rely even more so on assumptions, only to find ourselves having to backtrack on many occasions in order to get back on track so we can move forward. How many of us assume that all the information that we gather on the Internet is correct? What about those people that we meet online in our chat rooms or online dating services— do we just assume they are really whom they claim to be? This age of high technology and the warp speed we find ourselves operating in will, at times, have us make assumptions where we really need to be careful. You'll find that I'm even careful on the phone, even though I have caller ID and always identify myself (and ask the caller to do the same), just to be sure.

We constantly have to remind ourselves that nothing is wrong with pausing for a moment, and instead of making assumptions, asking ourselves the pertinent questions that will give us the real answers. For example, with the Internet, don't just take the word of the first website you visit. Do your research by looking for information on the topic in question on several websites to see whether they agree, and if they disagree, question the reliability of the source and investigate further until you have informed knowledge on the subject, rather than just an assumption you made or the assumption of one potentially unreliable website.

The best tried and true method to work with in regards to assumptions about our relationships and other people is to sit down and have a meaningful discussion...and yes, you got it, ask the hard questions. That solution, unfortunately, is precisely what many of us don't want to do because we often don't know or want to know the answer or reason for a situation we've decided to make an assumption about; we may prefer the answer we have in our head, or we may just be lazy and not want to invest the time, patience, and listening skills required to find out the truth.

Personally, I believe effective communication is always the best solution. That's when you really take the time to ask the question, but even more importantly, implement effective listening into the process. The old saying, "God gave us two eyes, two ears, and one mouth...and we should use them in that ratio" should be put into practice here. How many times do we find ourselves chomping at the bit to say something right in the middle of a conversation when someone else is speaking? We can't wait to get in our little "two cents worth" while the words being spoken to us are not even registering.

You may find this hard to believe, especially if you've ever seen me give a speech in front of a crowd of thousands of people, but basically, I'm an introvert. I have learned to force myself, when appropriate, to become an extrovert (or at least a lot more outgoing). Because I'm generally fairly quiet, I don't know how many times over the years I've been told, "James, you're a really good listener." I do tend to listen a lot more than I talk for a couple of reasons, (1) I usually am really interested in what people are saying, (2) I'm not interested in seeing who can win the battle of words or to show how smart I may or may not be, (3) and I like to use some advice I heard many years ago, "Seek first to understand, then be understood." At the end of a conversation, I tend to know a lot more about the other person than he or she knows about me, precisely because I focused on listening rather than talking.

I used to have a basketball coach years ago who would write the word "assume" in big letters on the chalkboard and then break down the word to show us what it often can mean. He'd say, "When you assume, you make an "ass" out of "u" and "me." Not only is that a clever play on words, but it's so true. There's not a lot of room for assumptions in a fast-paced game of basketball. You can't just assume that your teammate is going to read your mind without you communicating to him in a way he'll understand. If you are the point guard dribbling down court at a breakneck speed, you only have a split second to communicate to your teammate where you're going to pass the ball, and if you mis-communicate, you end up with either a turnover, the ball sailing out of bounds, or even more embarrassing, the ball hitting your teammate upside the head because he wasn't looking at you. Communication comes in all forms, and on the basketball court, we need to use every bit of it (body language, signals, looks, words, and everything else it takes to communicate). One of the reasons why basketball players learn to communicate in so many different ways is because it's hard to rely solely on verbal communication in front of 20,000 screaming fans. For communication to be effective, everyone involved has to be on the same page, and that's true not just in basketball, but in all areas of life.

In the end, making assumptions is never going to be as productive as effective communication. Saying what needs to be said, asking questions that need to be asked, and listening to what others have to say, without jumping to assumptions, is going to make life easier and better for everyone involved.

ALWAYS DO YOUR BEST

You may have noticed that all these agreements are hard to keep individually without keeping them all; at least, they are all closely connected, and "Always Do Your Best" sort of sums them all up.

This last agreement sounds simple, doesn't it? But when you think about it, how often do we really, truly do our best? In just about every situation we've ever had, if we had a chance to do it all over again, wouldn't we most likely change something to make it better? How often can we say we gave 100 percent of our best effort to complete the task at hand, whether it was work-related, or developing and maintaining a relationship?

Always doing your best requires always being on top of your game and giving 100 percent effort. One of the things I've learned over the years is that I may not always win every situation, but in every situation, I can always walk away feeling good from knowing I gave it my best shot.

For example, I didn't win my run for the office of Mayor for the City of Seattle in 2009, but as a "newbie" in the world of politics, I gave it my best shot and felt good about my efforts when it was all behind me, and coming in fourth place out of eight candidates was pretty good considering my level of experience and the quality of some of the competition. So I felt that, all in all, I had a pretty good showing. It just goes to show you that even if you just commit to doing your best, you never know where you may end up. If you never try it, you will never have a chance.

Therefore, no matter the situation, no matter who you're dealing with, whether it's work, family, friendships, homework, being a friendly neighbor, athletics, or any other situation, the question always to ask yourself is: Am I doing my best?

Several years ago, I had the opportunity to hear the Rev. Jesse Jackson give a sermon at my church home, Mount Zion Baptist Church. One thing that really stood out for me in Rev. Jackson's sermon was when he said, "If we do our best, God will do the rest." I thought that was so beautiful and so apropos. Just think about it—doing our best doesn't mean we're going to be the best at what we do, but it does mean we are placed in the best position possible for us to be successful.

Recently when I spoke to a group of young middle school children, I encouraged them to make at least one promise to themselves that they would actually be able to keep. That promise was that they would graduate from high school. I pointed out to them that in the state of Washington, 35 percent of all high school students drop out before graduation, and over 55 percent of children of color drop out of high school before graduation. Those numbers are outrageous and completely unacceptable! Once those students take themselves off the road of success, they'll have a more difficult time getting back onto it, if they ever do. So I told those kids at the very least to promise themselves (the promise automatically extends to their parents) that they would graduate from high school. By graduating from high school, a world of opportunities will open up for them. After graduation, they can pick and choose (depending on college criteria) which university they want to attend. They can pick and choose (depending on employment criteria) which jobs they want to apply for. They can pick and choose (depending on their own passions and skill sets) which career paths they want to pursue. Do you see what I'm getting at? Just by fulfilling the basic, simple promise to yourself to get a high school diploma, you've already greatly increased your odds of being successful.

Always doing our best is also vitally important when it comes to picking and choosing our life partners. One of the best relationship books I've read over the years is *Date or Soul Mate: How to Know if Someone is Worth Pursuing in Two Dates or Less* by Neil Clark Warren, the founder of the incredibly successful online matchmaking service eHarmony. The philosophical concepts Warren implements on eHarmony are the same ones he wrote about in his book. Determining compatibility is basically about paying attention to the warning signs and red flags we tend to ignore when we enter a relationship. In his book, Warren suggests that we create a list of "must haves" and a list of "can't stands" and keep that list in mind when we start pursuing someone we hope will be our lifelong partner. The idea is to fulfill as many of the "must haves" on the list as you possibly can, and to make sure you have as few checkmarks on the "can't stands" list as possible. Then at least you know what you're getting into. When you see those red flags become a reality (and most likely they will), they were on your "can't stands list" all along, and then you know to leave the relationship. Too often, we see the red flags right in front of us, but we talk ourselves into thinking things will change or that we can change the other person, so we continue the relationship. But ask yourself honestly, if you see red flags and you pursue the other person anyway, are you really doing the best you can, or are you just settling?

MAKING YOUR OWN PERSONAL AGREEMENTS

In addition to Ruiz's Four Agreements that I've talked about in this chapter, I've taken it upon myself to make a few additional personal agreements with myself. I think it's a good idea for all of us to have two or three additional personal agreements with ourselves in addition to the other four agreements discussed in this chapter.

When I was about ten years old, I experienced an interesting event that has really helped me to shape a couple of personal agreements that I've lived by ever since. These agreements have turned out to be a fantastic way for me to live my life, and they've kept me out of potentially danger-ous situations, especially when I was younger and more impressionable. The agreements I made with myself have helped me to build a strong character, but at the same time, not to judge others. These agreements have become principles by which I have lived my life.

That day when I was ten years old, I came home from school one after-noon to find my uncle sprawled across our couch in a drunken stupor. Now I don't know if you have a mom like I had, but my mom always had the living room furniture under plastic drop-cloths to preserve its cleanli-ness as much as possible. When you have four rough-and-tumble children growing up in a household (especially with children as big as we were), things tend to get broken, and if not broken, things tend to get worn out pretty quickly. The plastic drop-cloths on the furniture were there not only to protect the furniture, but also to impress upon us that there was no need to sit on the furniture (let alone jump on it) unless absolutely necessary, such as on those rare occasions when we had company.

So you can imagine my surprise when I found my drunk uncle lying on our couch. Being only ten, I didn't fully understand what was wrong with him. I knew he didn't smell good, and he didn't look so hot (all di-sheveled and dirty), and I could feel the hushed atmosphere in the house, one almost of embarrassment. I come from a family where neither my mom or dad drank alcohol of any sort (all right, all right...my mom did sip a little glass of wine every now and then...she said it was good for her blood), but we rarely had anyone come to our home and consume alco-hol in front of us. Once in a while at family gatherings, the grown-ups would bring a few six packs with them, but that was a very rare occasion. I really didn't know what was wrong until one of my parents whispered to me that my uncle was drunk. Then I felt a knot form in my stomach and my feet became glued to the floor as I stared at him in bewilderment, wondering whether he would ever come out of his stupor, or would he die right there in front of me? At that moment, I made a promise to myself that I would never be in that situation; I would never ever drink alcohol, I would never ever smoke, and I would never ever do drugs. All three of those promises came to me during that one impactful moment because my uncle was such a pitiful sight to me.

Because of those promises I made to myself, I've been able to withstand a tremendous amount of peer pressure at times when friends and team-mates became involved with drinking, drugs, or smoking. Whenever I was around any of those activities, I didn't feel even one ounce of temptation to indulge. I never put myself in a situation where I could say something as foolish as former President Bill Clinton—that I tried it but I didn't inhale—or that I drank but didn't get drunk. Ridiculous!

Because of my firm commitment to promises I made to myself, I've been able to stand tall in the face of those temptations. I can't even call them temptations because they don't even seem to register with my being. Those promises I made to myself I have every intention of keeping for the rest of my life. So when they break out the bubbly, I'll make sure it's the non-alcoholic type.

What promises are you going to make to yourself? If you're in school, will you promise yourself to finish school and graduate? If you tend to look for love in all the wrong places, will you promise yourself to take the steps necessary to make better choices? What steps will you promise yourself to take so you can make the best impression possible? Will you promise yourself to wait until after marriage to have a child? Will you promise to respect your spouse, and more importantly, respect yourself? Will you promise not to judge others based on their culture, background, language, or lifestyle? Will you promise actively to nurture the good relationships in your life? Will you promise yourself to leave a bad relationship? Will you promise to do things differently next time?

The questions and promises can go on and on, and because everyone reading this book is an individual, his or her situations and promises will vary. Only you know what you're going through and what you need to do better. Only you know what your temptations are, what you are strong in withstanding, and where you're weak.

Always doing your best involves knowing yourself first and foremost because only you know whether you are truly making a 100 percent effort. Your parents don't know, your teachers don't know, your coaches don't know, and your friends don't know...but you truly know. The last thing you want is to be kicking yourself and having regrets because you didn't push yourself just a little harder or you didn't apply yourself that little bit more that would have made all the difference. If you're applying for college and you need a 2.5, but you only have a 2.4, you can probably look back at the classes where you goofed off and realize that if you had only tried a little harder, you could have gotten that "B" instead of that "C," and then you'd be on your way to college.

We can look at virtually every situation we've dealt with in life and realize the places where we could have done just a little bit better. That's what always doing your best is all about. That's what making your own personal agreements with yourself is all about. Keeping those agreements with yourself helps you to create a platform you can operate from to enhance your chances of being successful and to enhance the quality of the life you're meant to enjoy.

It's up to you to live by the Four Agreements and your own personal agreements. Keep in mind that life is a journey full of ups and downs, trials and tribulations; at times there will be a lot of uncertainty where you will feel a lack of faith or confidence. But when you can look back on that road knowing you stuck to your principles and really made a 100 percent effort, you'll feel so much better, and you'll have a lot more to share with the folks who are traveling on that road right behind you.

Chapter 17

DANCE WITH MY FATHER

One of my all time favorite songs is Luther Vandross' "Dance with My Father." It's the only song that brings tears to my eyes every single time I hear it. If you don't know the song, I encourage you to search online for the lyrics or to buy the music. I don't know what kind of relationship Luther Vandross had with his father, but I can only hope that the song was inspired by his own personal experience of his father lifting him high and spinning him round and round before taking him up the stairs and tucking him in for a good night's sleep.

I love the song because it reminds me so much of my early childhood memories with my father. Not that he would spin me around until I fell asleep, but I remember how often he would send me off to bed after checking to see whether I had finished my homework and taken care of all my chores around the house. I respected my dad so much that just knowing he cared enough to check on me meant so much. My dad isn't the overly emotional type; in fact, he's always been the strong silent type (I don't think I've ever seen him shed a tear). He wasn't the type to take me out back and toss the ball with me or shoot hoops with me, but he was always around and he instilled in me all the qualities I would need to become the "fine young man" I grew up to be.

Men, and especially those of you who are fathers, I want you to remember this! You're not bad guys or bad people! Sure, we get portrayed as buffoons on TV, and we don't get a lot of respect at home or in any other walk of life, but we all have to remember that we have so much to offer and to give back to young people and to the wonderful relationships we have. We can do so much more, and whether we know it or not, we're being asked to do so much more. We're being asked to connect with our children, we're being asked to stay with our relationships, we're being asked to be leaders in our neighborhoods and communities. So many ways exist for us to feel good about the roles we play so we don't have to feel beaten down or defeated by a relationship that didn't work out or by children who never seem to respect us. Keep hanging in there and do your best!

In a wonderful article[1] in *Parade* magazine for Father's Day 2009, titled "We Need Fathers to Step Up," President Barack Obama urged all men to step up to their responsibilities, stating:

I observe this Father's Day not just as a father grateful to be present in my daughters' lives but also as a son who grew up without a father in my own life. My father left my family when I was two years old, and I knew him mainly from the letters he wrote and the stories my family told. And while I was lucky to have two wonderful grandparents who poured everything they had into helping my mother raise my sister and me, I still felt the weight of his absence throughout my childhood.

Wow! How many of us can relate to that same situation?

---

1 I encourage you to read the full article at http://www.parade.com/news/2009/06/barack-obama-we-need-fathers-to-step-up.html

President Obama went on to say:

> In many ways, I came to understand the importance of fatherhood through its absence—both in my life and in the lives of others. I came to understand that the hole a man leaves when he abandons his responsibility to his children is one that no government can fill. We can do everything possible to provide good jobs and good schools and safe streets for our kids, but it will never be enough to fully make up the difference.

> That is why we need fathers to step up, to realize that their job does not end at conception; that what makes you a man is not the ability to have a child but the courage to raise one.

The President sums up his thoughts by stating:

> As fathers, we need to be involved in our children's lives not just when it's convenient or easy, and not just when they're doing well—but when it's difficult and thankless, and they're struggling. That is when they need us most.

Most men don't have a lot of great things to say about their fathers for a variety of reasons. Perhaps the father wasn't around during the boy's growing up years, or maybe the boy felt abandoned or not appreciated by his dad. Maybe the father had an anger issue or substance abuse problem that caused holy terror to rain down upon the household. Whatever might be your situation, I challenge you to reach out to your dad and welcome him into your world.

I have a vision I can only hope plays out across the world one day where boys and grown men and their fathers will somehow reach out to each other and form much more meaningful relationships and bonds than they have ever done before. I can picture Luther Vandross' beautiful song playing in the background as every boy and man thinks back to how special his father was to him when he was only seven or eight years old—how he thought his father was his "superhero" who would protect him from all harm. I'm sure we can all recall how we would marvel that dad knew so many things we were curious about. I used to watch in amazement as my dad would fix the car, repair the fence, trim the hedges, paint a lawn chair, and mow the lawn all in one Saturday afternoon. He would even manage to give my brothers and me our Saturday afternoon haircuts (we had to get ready for church early!), and I can still remember the smell of the 3-in-1 oil he would use to lubricate his clippers.

A dad means so much to every young boy, and I feel for boys who either didn't have a dad around or have bad memories of when dad was around. Dads are definitely not perfect, and most dads really struggle in their roles as fathers, but you have to admire the ones who hang in there through it all. If you're a dad who happens to have a young son, pick him up and swing him around and around, and then carry him off to tuck him into bed. He'll know he's loved, and he'll never forget it!

In his book, *Better Dads, Stronger Sons*, Rick Johnson says that the relationship between a father and a son is like none other. Dads have a God-given role to protect and provide for their families, while always striving to teach their sons the life skills they'll need to grow into honorable men.

Because many dads struggle with feelings of inadequacy regarding their fathering abilities, Johnson shows how fathers can become equipped and inspired to be positive role models for their sons. He stresses the significance of male bonding, discipline, and spiritual leadership; he also emphasizes the importance of talking to your sons about such topics as sexual purity, respect, and self-discipline, and he reveals the "Top 10 Mistakes to Avoid as a Father."

From commitment and courage to honesty and humility, *Better Dads, Stronger Sons* helps men strive to be the dads God designed them to be—so their sons can grow to be everything they are meant to be.

Several other good books on fathers and sons have been published in recent years, including Tim Russert's *Big Russ and Me* and *Wisdom of Our Fathers: Lessons and Letters from Daughters and Sons.* Russert poignantly describes his relationships with his dad and his son with a sense of humor whiles telling stories of times they spent sharing joy, as well as sorrow and pain.

Remember when Bill Cosby was given the title "America's Favorite TV Dad" after his great portrayal of father Cliff Huxtable on *The Cosby Show*? Cosby had his own bestselling book *Fatherhood*, in which he brought a lot of humor to the role of being a father. He has some funny lines like "Fatherhood is...pretending the present you love most is soap-on-a-rope," and "helping your children learn English as a foreign language," or "knowing that 'Everything's okay, Dad' means 'I haven't killed anyone.'"

I'm not a father myself (yet), but I do hope that someday I will experience that blessing. I am a "father figure" to numerous young men and pride myself on being a positive role model. That gives me great satisfaction for now while I wait to see what the future holds for me. In the meantime, guys, keep stepping up to do the best you can by meeting the responsibilities you've been tasked with as men.

To conclude, here's a list of some things dads can do to connect with their sons:

- Talk to them about things that matter, not just sports, cars, and/or bragging about the women you desire.

- Hug them.

- Tell your sons you love them.

- Participate in their lives and interests.

- Listen.

- Take the initiative.

- Make the first move or call.

- Be pro-active.

- Ask them about the meaningful relationships in their lives.

- Let them be themselves.

- Acknowledge their accomplishments.

- Put time aside to spend with just them.

- Tell them stories about when you were a boy and your relationship with your father.

- Be accepting.

- Show the world that you're proud of them.

FINAL THOUGHTS

Thank you for taking the time to read this book and to listen to my stories and advice. You may have decided to read this book because you're a basketball fan, or you may have decided to read it to find some advice so you can improve your life. In either case, I hope I've given you a little entertainment and a lot to think about.

Most importantly, I hope I've encouraged you to live your life so you are the kind of person who can **Stand Above the Crowd**.

In closing, I want to say that if you only take one thing away from this book, I hope it will be that as long as you try to be your best…you'll be so much further along than if you never tried at all. Success is just around the corner for all of us who continue on the "pathway" of success. You can do it by deciding to make the best decisions possible that will keep you on your way to success. Remember, successful people are willing to do the extra things that unsuccessful people aren't willing to do.

Best wishes for your success,

James Donaldson

March 13, 2011

THE FIFTY GREATEST PLAYERS IN NBA HISTORY

The most frequently asked questions I encounter after "How tall are you?" are "Who is the *greatest* player you've ever played against?" and "Who is the *toughest* player you've ever played against?" Depending on who's asking the question and the person's knowledge of basketball, I typically give a couple of different responses. There's a big difference between "the greatest" and "the toughest."

The game of basketball has evolved a lot since 1891 when Dr. James Naismith first tied a peach basket to an old barn post and the players were shooting two-hand set shots. Today, the game is played on a global scale with some of the finest athletes in the world. There were great players back in the beginning of the game, just as there are great players now. I don't know if it's ever totally fair to compare players from one era with players of another. Periodically, you see sports aficionados coming up with hypothetical computerized scenarios of, say, the great Green Bay Packers of the 1960s versus the New England Patriots of the new millennium. It's impossible to really say who the best players are or which team would come out on top. But it's a fun exercise, and it creates a lot of heated conversations among sports fanatics and all of us.

I was lucky to play during perhaps the greatest era of NBA basketball. My NBA career spanned two decades essentially, 1980-1996. Some of the greatest NBA players ever to play the game were on the court during those years. I remember as a rookie in 1980 marveling at the incredible Dr. J. and I've also been able to witness the new era of NBA basketball that was brought to us by Ervin "Magic" Johnson, Larry Bird, and Michael Jordan.

All in all, I was privileged to play against over thirty of the all-time fifty greatest NBA players. I'm going to go through the whole list and share my thoughts with you in regards to having actually played against them or watching them while I was still a youngster. They are listed in alphabetical order, and if you want to find the actual numerical order in which they are listed by the NBA, you can check out its website at **www.NBA.com**

As a special addition, I've asked a couple of my mentors—Tom "Satch" Sanders, eight-time NBA champion with the Boston Celtics, and Lenny Wilkens, NBA Hall of Famer both as a player and coach—to contribute their real-life experiences to what it was like to play against some of the all-time greats of their era. I've placed their initials (LW or TS) after the players they've assisted me in writing about. Thanks, guys! I really appreciate you.

KAREEM ABDUL-JABBAR

I often tell the story of how as a rookie during my very first professional game playing for the Seattle SuperSonics in the Kingdome in Seattle, I was lined up against Kareem Abdul-Jabbar. Kareem was already a ten- to twelve-year established veteran and well on his way to becoming one of the greatest players ever to play the game. I remember checking into the game for just a few minutes and being given the instructions to go guard Kareem. As we were lining up on the foul line, I remember thinking to myself, "Wow, here is the great Kareem Abdul-Jabbar, and I'm going to have to figure out a way not to get embarrassed out here." I also remember thinking to myself, "Kareem already has over 20,000 points in his career and I've got zero."

It was truly one of my first tests as far as trying to establish myself as an NBA player. I was nervous as all-get-out, but after jostling with Kareem and "bodying" with him for a few minutes, I started to calm down and felt a little more comfortable.

In my estimation, Kareem was the most unstoppable player ever to play the game. With that fantastic skyhook of his, he could shoot and score at will and with great accuracy. There was nothing you could do to slow down Kareem other than hope and pray his teammates wouldn't feed him the ball all night long or that he was having an extremely rare night off…but that hardly ever happened.

So that's one variation of the question I'm asked as far as "Who's the toughest or greatest player you've ever played against?" I always answer that Kareem was the most unstoppable—hands-down!

NATE ARCHIBALD

I played against Nate "Tiny" Archibald at the tail end of his career. Since he was a point guard and I was a big center, we rarely matched up on the court. Nate was one of the great players in NBA history simply because of his uncanny ability to handle the ball, score, and dish out assists—always out there for his team.

Nate was always one of my favorite players to watch simply because he was so smooth and had such a cool demeanor. Check out his career statistics! He could do it all, especially from the point guard position.

PAUL ARIZIN (LW)

Paul Arizin was elected to the Naismith Memorial Basketball Hall of Fame in 1978 and was selected to the NBA All-Star team in each of the ten years he played in the league. He perfected the jump shot, which was relatively new at the time, and he was able to utilize screens better than anyone else in his era.

Paul was a pesky defensive player, a good ball handler, and he loved to run the court. He led the Philadelphia Warriors to the NBA Championship in 1956, and he was named one of the Fifty Greatest Players in NBA History in 1996.

CHARLES BARKLEY

Charles Barkley was a riot to play against. He was one of the guys who always had fun out there, yet because of his tremendous talent, he could dominate a game at both ends of the floor. Given the fact that he was only about 6'4" and weighed in at an impressive 250 pounds, he gave all of us big guys fits because of his quick leaping ability and great instincts for the ball. Because of his seemingly arrogant personality, Charles didn't consistently get the respect due to him throughout his career. But he definitely goes down as one of the all-time greats!

Charles is one of only two guys I can ever remember actually dunking on me; I challenged the shot with everything I had, yet I still got dunked on.

Actually, I don't feel too bad about it because he dunked on the whole team!

Here's how that moment played out. Charles was playing for the Philadelphia 76ers and I was playing with the San Diego Clippers. Charles was running the ball down the court at full speed, and he essentially took off from the foul line. He flew right by our point guard, Norm Nixon, and then he went by our shooting guard, Derek Smith. He kept right on coming past our small forward, Greg Kelser, and then past our power forward, Terry Cummings. He wasn't just going by them—he was going up and over them. I saw all this play out as if in slow motion, and by the time I reacted to what was going on, Charles was already halfway down the lane and past three of our guys. I jumped with all I could to challenge his shot as the last line of defense before the basket, but Charles just kept rising up and over me too, and he threw the ball down to the basket with such terrific force that it just brought the house down. If it hadn't been such a "fantastic moment," it probably would've been one of the most embarrassing moments for me on the basketball court. When you play against the best, such as a great player like Charles, you can't help but admire some of the things the best players can do on the basketball court. Besides, such moments are what the fans come to see!

RICK BARRY

I played against Rick Barry right at the end of his career; even then he was an amazing player as far as being able to shoot and score from just about anywhere and anytime on the court. One of my "big man" coaches in Dallas, Clifford Ray, was a teammate with Rick on the 1975 NBA Champion Golden State Warriors, so he would tell me great stories of how Rick could just take over games and "will" them to victory time and time again.

Rick was a phenomenal shooter from the foul line too, and guess what? He shot underhanded at over an amazing 90 percent!

ELGIN BAYLOR (LW)

Elgin Baylor starred at Seattle University before joining the Minneapolis Lakers. No player at that time defied gravity the way Elgin did. He literally looked like he was floating in the air.

With his uncanny ability to change hands and direction while in mid-air, Elgin was way ahead of his time by performing amazing feats in the courts that weren't seen on a regular basis until the likes of Connie Hawkins, Julius "Dr. J" Erving, and Michael Jordan.

At one point in his career, Elgin scored over 23,000 points while reaching the NBA finals seven times in a nine-year period. Amazing!

He was an eleven-time NBA All-Star and enshrined as a Hall of Famer in 1977.

DAVE BING (TS)

Detroit's Dave Bing was a special kind of player. He appeared to space out his scoring to the point where you didn't know he was accumulating such great numbers. What you did know was that if you passed the ball anywhere near him, he would make the steal and be on his way to scoring an easy basket. Bing had extraordinarily quick hands. The term "quiet but deadly" comes to mind when describing Dave Bing's game.

LARRY BIRD

Larry was the "real deal" as far as a guy coming into the league and being as great in the NBA (Boston Celtics) as he was in college (Indiana State). He played hard every night and commanded the respect of everyone on the floor. I admired his tenacity and his "guts" in trash talking and backing it up every time.

I remember when Larry came to play the Dallas Mavericks on his through-Texas swing of games against Dallas, Houston, and San Antonio, and he lit all three teams up by averaging over forty points a game. He tagged fifty on us!

WILT CHAMBERLAIN (TS)

Wilt helped put Philadelphia and San Francisco on the sports map back in his day. In fact, Wilt Chamberlain changed the "wish list" of many NBA owners who thought having an awesome point scoring machine was going to be the answer to their NBA championship dreams.

Wilt's incredible 100 point scoring binge during his 50.2 points per game average in the 1962 season had everyone's attention. The 7'3," 275-pound superstar was the talk of the NBA. Wilt was one of the greatest attractions the NBA ever had as well as being a gifted player.

BOB COUSY (TS)

Bob Cousy was the "Mr. Basketball" of his time and he carried the deserved title well. This Boston Celtic great played the game with grand style and plenty of ball-handling magic. He was instrumental in helping the Celtics win their first few NBA Championships.

We're talking about a player here who set early assist records and found a way to score with one-handed push shots, left- and right-handed running hook shots, and underhand scoops. Bob Cousy was a show to watch in action.

DAVE COWENS

Dave Cowens was always one of my favorite Boston Celtics throughout the years. That was probably because of a number of things I saw in him and his game that I really connected to. He wasn't the most talented player on the court, and he wasn't the biggest and strongest guy either. But he had more than enough determination and intensity to make up for whatever shortcomings he had, through pure hustle and an all-out passion for the game. There are some great NBA highlight reel videos that show Dave Cowens chasing down loose balls and sliding twenty or thirty feet across the court in order to do so. You just don't see that many guys playing that way!

Another thing I remember about Dave Cowens was that he seemed to be a consummate team player. He didn't care how many points he scored or how many rebounds he had, but he seemed to give everything he had every time he was on the court. And another thing, he wasn't afraid to get into his teammates' faces (if he felt they weren't giving it their all) and I never ever saw him back down from anybody else. Those are the kinds of guys you want to go to war with any day of the week!

BILLY CUNNINGHAM (TS)

Billy C" was a left-handed, high-jumping forward with good ball-handling skills. His deceptively quick moves to the basket allowed the "Kangaroo Kid" to dunk on many opponents.

The Philadelphia fans were in love with the excitement that was generated when Cunningham began one of his one-on-one moves to the basket, and then he would pull up for a soft close-range jumper. The fans knew then that the stage was set for his next move to go all the way to the basket.

DAVE DEBUSSCHERE (TS)

Dave DeBusschere was an ideal forward. The Detroit Pistons and New York Knickerbockers player was able to score from twenty to twenty-five feet and then take an opponent strongly to the basket. He was a tough rebounding and defensive player and was clearly one of the best all-around forwards ever to play the game. His contributions definitely helped the NY Knicks get to the NBA Championship rounds time and again.

CLYDE DREXLER

As a fan of basketball, you have to love Clyde "The Glide" Drexler. He was one of those "silent assassins." He went about his job on the court with such smoothness and efficiency that sometimes you wouldn't realize how dominating his performance was.

Clyde was one of the pure class gentlemen of the league, yet at the same time a ferocious competitor. In the late 1980s when I played for the Dallas Mavericks, our games against Drexler and his Portland Trailblazer team turned in some outstanding performances and games. I'd have my hands full guarding the Portland big guys in the lane, and Clyde would be right in there battling with all of us for rebounds and involved in physical plays in the paint. You don't see that too often from your superstar guys, who typically are the most talented players on the court and can get away with not getting their noses bloodied.

Like a lot of great players from that era, Clyde would have been talked about as an all-time great in every basketball conversation if it hadn't been for some of the other faces of the NBA at the time, à la Magic Johnson, Larry Bird, Dr. J, and Michael Jordan.

JULIUS ERVING

Ah…where do you start with Julius "Dr. J." Erving? You start right at the top of the list, that's where you start!

Dr. J. was one of those iconic players that we kids growing up in the early '70s would just marvel at whenever we got a chance to catch a glimpse of him on TV. Back then, Dr. J. was playing for the American Basketball Association (ABA), and until there was serious talk about a possible ABA/NBA merger, he was almost a mythical and mystical basketball marvel doing fabulous things in the ABA that many guys in the NBA only dreamed of doing.

Not only do I put Dr. J. up there as one of my all-time favorite players, but I also list him as one of the true greats of the game. He was someone who carried the heavy mantle of representing the ABA and all its glorious players and tried to elevate that league to a place where up until then the NBA had claimed sole supremacy.

I remember seeing Dr. J. in person for the first time as a rookie in 1980 when the team I was on at the time, the Seattle SuperSonics, was on a road trip and we pulled into the hotel in Milwaukee to prepare for our game against the Bucks a night or two later. Dr. J. and his team, the

Philadelphia 76ers, were checking out of the hotel just as we were check-ing in. I remember being in almost a state of playful giddiness along with a couple of other rookies on the team at the time, Vinnie Johnson and James Bailey, because we were all excited to see Dr. J. and the Philadelphia 76ers…up close and in person!

Dr. J. seems to be in a class all by himself and he had a way of standing out in every crowd he was in—whether he was on the court or walking through a hotel lobby. He was one of the few guys in the league I really wanted to pattern my demeanor and personality after because of his very professional approach to the game, on and off the court.

PATRICK EWING

There's a very short list of players who played with the tenacity Patrick Ewing played with throughout his entire career. There have been those players who played hard and ferocious because they were trying to make up for lack of talent, but Patrick had tremendous talent and still played with a fire and determination that inspired the rest of his team.

Patrick doesn't get nearly the recognition and respect due him for almost single-handedly carrying a New York Knicks team that was routinely overmatched in the talent department in all the key positions, except for center. He became even more of a force to be reckoned with when he was coached by Pat Riley, who had a way of bringing out the best in all his players…or you just weren't going to play, no matter how good you thought you were.

I was fortunate to be a teammate of Patrick Ewing for a short time during the 1991-92 season after I was traded to the New York Knicks from the Dallas Mavericks. I got to see for myself up close and personal the preparation, determination, leadership, and consistency that Patrick brought to his team. Patrick is one of the classic examples of an all-time great falling just short of an NBA championship ring, and that just goes to show you that sometimes it's the luck of the draw and basketball is still a team game even when your team has one of the top five players of that era.

I mention to people from time to time those players whom I would welcome into "the foxhole" if we had to fight our way out of any situation in the heat of battle. Patrick Ewing tops the list!

WALT FRAZIER (TS)

Walt "Clyde" Frazier was a guard of unusual skills. Unusual in the sense that he seldom beat his opponents with speed; instead, he used deceptive ball-handling skills and a strong body to keep players from stopping his penetration to the basket or bothering him while he was hitting his medium-range jump shot.

Frazier was known for his playing style as he played the passing lanes better than most. He also brought a certain style to his off-the-court attire and carriage. He was the starting point guard on both New York Knick Championship teams of the 1970s.

GEORGE GERVIN

George "Ice" Gervin was a marvel to watch on the basketball court. So smooth with every movement, he would tantalize you into watching him so you didn't dare over-commit yourself to trying to stop one move, because he would come right back with another one on you. He had a variety of great shots that were virtually unstoppable, including a mid-range jump shot from about every angle on the court, bank shots from just about every angle (he would actually call out "bank" as he shot the ball), and, of course, as everyone knows, "George could finger roll."

They called him "Ice" because of his ultra-cool demeanor on the court. I remember an awesome poster at the time in which George was sitting on huge cubes of ice that were fashioned as a throne, bedecked in a robe and crown, with a basketball in hand. It was one of the best posters of the day and all the guys thought it was so cool.

Gervin played for the San Antonio Spurs throughout the majority of his career. The Spurs were always one of my favorite teams to play against because not only did it have Gervin, but it also had one of my favorite point guards in James Silas, and the biggest, strongest player in the league that I had to go up against—Artis "A–Train" Gilmore. I wasn't privy to all the locker room chemistry that may or may not have been there with these opponents, but they always seemed to be a team that had fun on the basketball court, and we matched up against them pretty well.

HAL GREER (TS)

Philadelphia's sharp shooting guard, Hal Greer, was a perfectionist. He only shot when it was a good opportunity for him or his team. No forcing shots for him. He shot only one shot, whether he was in the offense or on the foul line. This great mid-range scorer made it almost impossible to double-team Wilt Chamberlain. The ball would be swung to Greer by either Chamberlain or another teammate, and the high percentage shooting guard would sink it. Greer was a very important player during the 76er's Championship team.

JOHN HAVLICEK (TS)

John Havlicek was known as the best "6th man" ever to play the game. This Boston Celtic forward utilized his exceptional stamina to run opponents into the ground and then would abuse them with all kinds of scoring shots. His very quick hands on defense saved the Celtics in many a game. He played his heart out for many years on several Celtic NBA Championship teams.

ELVIN HAYES

I was fortunate to play against Elvin "Big E" Hayes throughout the early part of my career, or perhaps I should say, fortunately I only had to play against Elvin "Big E" Hayes the early part of my career. I came into the NBA in 1980 and Elvin retired in 1983, so I only had to play against him a couple of times a year, first when he was with the Houston Rockets and I was with the Seattle SuperSonics, and later at the end of his career.

Elvin was a forerunner of the big guys who played center. He could do a lot of different things on the basketball court. Elvin played the four position (power forward), but he was so versatile and interchangeable that he could move around on the basketball court wherever he needed to be effective. Plus, he played alongside Wes Unseld, who at 6'7" compared to Elvin's 6'10," was able to hold down the center position in the paint as well as any of the top centers of the day.

I tell the story often of how Elvin Hayes, and his bookend counterpart, Wes Unseld, gave me my first real introduction into life in the NBA. We were playing a game in Seattle against the Washington Bullets my rookie year. I swear to this day that I saw both Elvin and Wes communicating on how one was going to "take me high," and the other was going to "take me low" and on the very next play that's just what happened. I went up for a rebound, and before I knew it, my body had leveled out about six feet up in the air with Wes taking out my legs underneath and Elvin pushing me over from up top. I hit the ground with a tremendous thud that left me black and blue for weeks. It seemed to happen in slow motion, and in the time that it took me to hit the ground, the thought that went through my mind was *I can either tuck in my tail and run back to the bench looking for sympathy, or I can pick myself up, dust myself off, and hang in there with the big boys.* I chose the latter and I'm glad I did because I feel that was a defining moment in my young career. Not only did I hit the ground with a tremendous thud, but neither Elvin nor Wes even offered a hand to help me up off the ground. That was cold! But that was life in the NBA, especially for a young upstart like me.

ERVIN "MAGIC" JOHNSON

I first remember playing against Ervin "Magic" Johnson in 1979 at the Far West Classic basketball tournament in Portland, Oregon. I remember him being so exuberant, full of energy and excitement even back then as a freshman. He had a way of getting his teammates all caught up in the excitement of playing a game that's "supposed to be fun."

Never has there been a player who brought as much fun to the game and had as much talent and fan appeal as Magic Johnson. With his effervescent smile and magnificent ball handling and passing skills, he was "Mr. Showtime." He was usually the difference maker out there on the court when his team went against yours. On any given night, he was capable of putting up a "triple double," but I truly believe he derived much more pleasure helping his teammates to be better than they ever thought they could be…and he played with pretty darn good players!

Magic was all about "winning" and having fun, as he would say. He was a tremendous leader on the court at getting his players where he wanted them to be most effective and to enhance their odds of winning. I think people forget how truly talented Magic Johnson was because he played with so many incredibly talented players throughout his career. His Showtime Lakers teams of the 1980s were some of the most star-studded teams ever to grace the NBA.

Just look at the awesome lineup they were able to put on the floor throughout that decade with Jabbar, Worthy, Scott, Cooper, Nixon, and others! As always, I had my hands full with Jabbar, and I think Magic would "rub it in" from time to time by calling the play that was set for Jabbar "fist down," over and over again throughout the course of the game. I used to cringe and say, "Here we go again" as Jabbar would get himself into position and Magic would dribble on over and dump it down into the post for Jabbar to do his thing. Whether Jabbar scored or not, that play alone had a way of tying our defense into knots and putting us back on our heels.

You gotta take your hat off to Magic Johnson because he goes down in the history books not only as one of the all-time greats (top five in *my* book), but also the greatest at making his teammates better...and having a whole heck of a lot of fun doing it.

SAM JONES (TS)

Sam Jones was first known for his defensive prowess as he partnered with K.C. Jones as the "attack guys" on the Boston Celtics man-to-man press. That defensive focus lasted for three seasons; then "the real" Sam Jones emerged.

Players like Oscar Robertson and Jerry West will tell anyone willing to listen that Sam Jones was the best shooter in the game. With his range from medium to thirty feet, Sam Jones was unstoppable when he chose to be a "power shooter." The Boston Celtics owed a lot to the scoring prowess of the 6'4" Jones.

MICHAEL JORDAN

It seemed like year after year throughout the 1980s, another great player was coming into the NBA to elevate the game to an even higher level. It started with Larry Bird and Magic Johnson, and then a whole flood of great players such as Ewing, Olajuwon, Barkley, Malone, Stockton, Dominique, and more. Even with those household names, one stood out more than the rest—Michael Jordan.

Michael was flat-out pure talent when he came into the league with a dazzling array of jump shots, drives to the basket, and fantastic dunks that we hadn't seen the likes of since a young Dr. J.

Michael's early years were ones where he was an unstoppable machine and evoked fear in every team in the league. I always felt bad for the two guards (shooting guards) who were assigned to guard him on the teams I played with as we prepared to play against the Chicago Bulls. Our whole game plan was structured to try to stop Michael Jordan, or at least slow him down.

Michael was the best talent in the league, but when he started winning championships, he became the best all-around player too. He had a way of making his teammates (very average teammates in many cases) much better than they actually were as they would get into position either to be decoys or legitimate threats once he got the ball to them.

A lot of great players were around during that era, but none commanded the total team's respect more than Michael Jordan. When I lay everything out side by side by side (championships, scoring titles, and overall statistics), Michael Jordan has to go down as the greatest NBA player ever.

JERRY LUCAS (LW)

Jerry Lucas was not the most athletic player in the NBA, but he was relentless in striving for perfection. His goal was to be the best rebounder at that time. He averaged over seventeen rebounds a game for the Cincinnati Royals.

Jerry could also score inside/outside and was an excellent passer. His ability to be a complete player made him very valuable to his teams, and he was one of the most rugged rebounders ever to play the game.

In 1965, he was voted as the NBA All-Star MVP of the annual NBA All-Star game.

KARL MALONE

In my book, Karl "The Mailman" Malone has to go down as one of the hardest-working, most talent-laden superstars who continued to work on and improve his game every year he was in the league. As a rookie from Louisiana Tech, Karl was a very good player, but perhaps more of an athlete than an overall basketball player. He could run and jump with the best of them, even at 6'9" and about 260 pounds. He kept working on his game until he got to a point where he was an excellent foul shooter (his first couple of years in the league his foul shooting was very limited), and he could pull up and hit a mid-range jumper from anywhere on the floor. He had blazing speed that would leave all of the other big men in the dust, and he could finish off his layups with thunderous tomahawk dunks (many times with his non-layup hand placed behind the back of his head as he posed for the flurry of flashbulbs that would go off while he was in mid-air finishing one of his dunks).

Consistency was the name of the game for Karl Malone. You could always count on him for his twenty points and ten rebounds night after night, year after year. You don't end up as the second-leading scorer in NBA history by just showing up; you have to work at it and be consistent.

I had many opportunities to play against the Karl Malone-led Utah Jazz over the years, and I would do my best to make sure Karl wouldn't take over the inside of the paint and dominate a game.

My last NBA stop was with the Utah Jazz where I was honored to be Karl's teammate. He kept the bar set really high for all of his teammates; we would hit the weight room before and after practice, and he didn't take too kindly to our not pushing ourselves as hard as we could. Karl was definitely one of those guys I wouldn't hesitate to go to battle with to take on any situation that confronted us.

MOSES MALONE

The types of centers that gave me the most difficulty were the ones who were a little bit smaller than me, just as strong, and super-quick. That was Moses Malone. On top of that, he was an extremely hard worker who never seemed to tire! Moses would go down in my book as the most difficult player for my position to play against over the years. He would just keep coming at you every single minute of the game and could play real solid defense on the other end (a trait for which he doesn't get much recognition). I knew going into a game playing against Moses Malone that it was going to be a long night, no matter who came out on top.

The game I remember most with Moses Malone was when I was with the Seattle SuperSonics and we played against his Houston Rockets in the playoffs. This was during my second or third year, but I was in the starting lineup most nights and playing a lot of minutes in the rotation just about every night. Jack Sikma was the starting center, and I was the backup center. Moses wore out both Jack and me to the tune of thirty-eight points and thirty-two rebounds! Every NBA player has a game he can remember in which his opponent just went off on him and there was absolutely nothing he could do. That playoff game back in 1983 was that game for me (and I'm sure for Jack too).

PETE MARAVICH (LW)

Pete was an outstanding player at Louisiana State University where he averaged an astounding forty-three points a game...as a freshman!!!

He was so dazzling and creative with the ball that at times he fooled not only the opponents, but also his own teammates with passes that would sometimes catch them unaware.

Fans loved his behind-the-back passes, fade-away jumpers, and his crazy-looking shots. Pete had such a flair and love for the game, and his style left such a lasting impact on basketball, that players such as Magic Johnson, Deron Williams, Steve Nash, Chris Paul, Derek Rose, Tony Parker, and many others attribute their playing styles to "Pistol Pete" Maravich.

KEVIN MCHALE

Kevin McHale had to be one of the smartest players I ever played against. His overall court brilliance really shone, especially when teamed with Larry Bird and Robert Parrish to form a formidable trio at both ends of the court. Kevin wasn't the most athletic player, but he seemed to have an uncanny knack for rebounds, key blocks, scoring, and defense just when his team needed it most.

The Boston Garden is the one arena throughout the whole NBA where I personally never tasted the thrill of victory, but tasted the agony of defeat every single time I played there. Kevin was a big part of that because he was a perfect complement for the rest of the great Boston Celtics teams that played there throughout that era.

GEORGE MIKAN (TS)

George Mikan was the defining center for professional basketball. At 6'10", this Minneapolis Lakers star player was a dominating figure who helped bring many NBA Championships to his team.

Mikan's low post attack with his swinging left and right-handed hook shots determined the outcome for any game in which he played. This celebrated player was the headliner wherever he performed and his prominence helped to establish the very young NBA professional league.

EARL MONROE (TS)

Earl "The Pearl" Monroe literally spun his way into the hearts of basketball fans everywhere. His on-balance spins and pirouettes on his way to scoring a great number of points made him a schoolyard legend as well as one of the most copied guards ever to play in the NBA. His play helped to make the Baltimore Bullets very competitive while, later on, this same super-talented player helped the New York Knicks to a championship.

HAKEEM OLAJUWON

Just when I was fortunate enough to start playing better against Moses Malone—who was starting to slow down a bit, or was playing on teams that weren't that great—along came Hakeem "The Dream" Olajuwon. No offense to Moses (and I'm sure he won't take any since he was Hakeem's mentor), but Hakeem was everything Moses was except he was packaged like a new and improved model. He worked just as tirelessly as anybody I've ever played against, but he had incredible athletic talent and developed into one of the most gifted big men ever. His "dream shake" was something that any opponent dreaded being humiliated by in a highlight video. Sometimes, your feet would either be glued to the ground because he would catch you off guard, or you would trip over yourself trying to keep up with him and his quick balletic moves.

During the early years of Hakeem's career, he was teamed with All-Star and fellow seven-footer Ralph Sampson; they were the "Twin Tower" concept that gave every team in the league a great deal of difficulty. But guess what? Hakeem became even better after Sampson was traded away. He led the Rockets to back-to-back championships. It was against Hakeem and the Rockets that I had the most serious injury of my career. I ruptured my patella tendon in my right knee as Hakeem and I were battling for a rebound. I went down in a heap and had to be carried off by about eight players on a stretcher to the locker room. Hakeem came by the locker room after the game to check on me and always seemed to check in on me every time I saw him throughout my long months of physical therapy rehabilitation.

Hakeem was always a gentleman no matter how hard you played and how physical you might be against him. I think he always knew he had the upper hand because of his tremendous gifts and his determination to be a winner. I'll never forget his mantra during his championship years with the Houston Rockets in the mid-1980s; he would repeat over and over during his interviews that he and his team would "stay humble and work hard." Wow, what a lesson to follow in everything we do!

SHAQUILLE O'NEAL

I played against Shaquille O'Neal his first couple of years in the league when he was still with the Orlando Magic. He was a pure physical specimen who had tremendous physical gifts and could dominate a game at will. I was at the tail-end of my career as I wrapped up my season with the Utah Jazz as a thirty-six-year-old backup journeyman center. I remember playing against Shaquille at a game in Orlando where I was able to hold my own against him physically. He turned and looked at me and said I was one of the strongest players he had to play against, and "By the way, how old are you?" he asked. When I told him I was thirty-six, he said, "Man, you won't catch me out here playing at thirty-six. I'm going to be chillin' on the beaches of Maui." Well, when I last checked in 2011, Shaquille O'Neal was still out there playing and making a run at another championship.

Shaquille grew into one of the most dominant players (and big men) of his era. No one could handle him one-on-one, and when he played with the Los Angeles Lakers, he would become a three-time NBA Champion and turn in magnificent performance after magnificent performance in dominating anyone matched up against him. He would routinely put up numbers such as thirty points (sometimes forty points) and twenty rebounds and lead his team to victory, all the while having a blast. At last count, he had four NBA Championship rings…will he get one for the thumb?

ROBERT PARISH

Robert Parish was known around basketball circles simply as "The Chief." Always serious and seldom cracking a smile, Robert "Chief" Parish was one of the dominant big men of his era, especially when he teamed up with Kevin McHale and Larry Bird with the Boston Celtics to form one of the most effective and dominant front lines throughout the 1980s.

When we played against the Boston Celtics, I would be matched up against Parish; he was always a handful for me because of his versatility and agility. A very smart and cagey player, but most importantly, completely unselfish, he would routinely take the second or third role in that trio and perform all the little nuances of the game that help a team to win.

The Celtics were completely loaded at all five positions with Dennis Johnson at point, Danny Ainge, shooting guard, Larry Bird at small forward, Kevin McHale at big forward, and the Chief anchoring down the middle. Parish was probably one of the all-time best starting five in NBA history, and that's with the Showtime Lakers around!

As I mentioned before, the Boston Garden is the one arena throughout the whole NBA where I never won a single game. Oh, we came close from time to time, but, as the saying goes, close only counts in horseshoes and hand grenades. "The Chief" was a big part of the success of the Celtics and one of the main reasons I never won a game at Boston Garden.

BOB PETTIT (TS)

This great St. Louis Hawks forward was the best example of a talented player who played well within his abilities. Bob Pettit set the example for many a young player who wanted to showcase talents he thought he had at the expense of the team, but could not help the team to win.

Pettit was the consummate professional. He could score points from eighteen feet and in range, and he seemingly rebounded every single shot that was missed. No extra dribbles, no tricky passes. Just a scoring and rebounding machine specialist. He took his St. Louis Hawks team to the playoffs and the finals many times, culminating in an NBA Championship. Bob Pettit was indeed a "Pro's Pro."

SCOTTIE PIPPEN

Throughout NBA history, all the top-flight superstar players always seem to be accompanied by a player who is almost as good (meaning better than everyone else on the team, except the superstar) and who doesn't mind taking a backseat to the superstar, because the game is all about winning. Teams loaded with two or three superstars on the court at the same time seldom win multiple NBA championships (Chamberlain, West, and Baylor of the Lakers, and Dr. J., George McGinnis, and Lloyd "World" Free of the star-studded Philadelphia 76ers come to mind right away). The latest team to try to win a championship by rounding up the most talent in the league is the Miami Heat. They've got LeBron James,

Dwayne Wade, and Chris Bosh on one team. We'll see how many championships they actually win.

Scottie Pippen epitomized what playing alongside a true superstar and winning championships is all about. He teamed with Michael Jordan on the six NBA championships that the Chicago Bulls won. Rarely did he actually have to carry the team, but he was so good that you had to watch him just as much as you had to watch and defend Michael Jordan. They complemented each other perfectly; Jordan was the very best player in the league at the time, and Pippen was in the top ten, if not the top five in the league.

Pippen did it all as far as being able to play every position on the floor—pass the ball, defend the ball, shoot the ball. He played unselfishly as the second half of that dynamic duo of Jordan and Pippen. There's no question who was the better player between the two of them, but for Pippen to be ranked in the top fifty all-time greatest NBA players, it was all about submerging his incredible talent and blending it into a team concept. The outcome...six NBA championship rings! Not many players can say that!

WILLIS REED (TS)

Willis Reed, known as "The Captain," was the tower of strength for the Championship New York Knicks teams of the 1970s. This left-handed, 6'9," 250-pound center/forward was a force to be reckoned with on the boards and in the offensive flow.

When Reed played the center position, his medium range shooting drew the opponent's center away from the basket, which created easy scoring opportunities underneath the basket for his cutting teammates. When he played the forward position, he took advantage of the average forward in the pivot and used his strong post moves to score. This versatile player was one of the best all-around players ever to don a New York Knicks uniform.

OSCAR ROBERTSON (TS)

The "Big O," as he was called, is considered by many as the best basketball player ever to have played the game. His almost four consecutive seasons averaging a "triple double" (that's double figures in points, rebounds, and assists) are the most impressive statistics against those of any other player who ever played.

Oscar Robertson led the Cincinnati Royals to the playoffs year after year as a high scoring, league wide assist leader point guard. However, it was his teaming up with Kareem Abdul-Jabbar that finally got him a championship ring. "Big O" was the complete and consummate player.

DAVID ROBINSON

David "The Admiral" Robinson was a class act! A graduate of the United States Naval Academy, Robinson conducted himself on and off the court with strict discipline and military precision.

Year after year, Robinson almost singlehandedly kept the San Antonio Spurs competitive. He could score with the best of them, run the floor incredibly well for a big man, rebound, block shots, and play defense unerringly!

Robinson was that first wave of "modern" big men who came into the league able to do many more things than just play in the pivot. Robinson's favorite shot was a face up twelve- to fifteen-footer. But if you tried to defend him too closely, he'd drive right around you for a tomahawk slam.

Robinson once put up an incredible seventy-plus points in an NBA game as he was going for the NBA scoring title. That's the kind of versatility and talent David Robinson had.

Dave Robinson was always a gentleman on and off the court, which made him a player I enjoyed competing against.

BILL RUSSELL (TS)

Bill Russell was the man most responsible for the eleven Boston Celtics NBA Championships in his thirteen seasons as a player. This 6'9" center took full advantage of his left-handed prowess to score, rebound, and lead his team to as many victories as it took to dominate thoroughly the Championship scene.

Bill Russell's shot blocking changed the NBA game. He mastered the art of not only blocking a shot, but keeping it in play and starting the fast break with it. In fact, Bill Russell's defensive play helped a few players decide to retire prematurely. Bill Russell is the player that many general managers agree would be their choice as the first player to select if they were starting a franchise. Now, that's quite a compliment!

DOLPH SCHAYES (TS)

Syracuse's Dolph Schayes was one of the hardest-working star forwards in the NBA's early years. When this forward broke his right arm, he proceeded to perfect his left hand during the off-season. He then performed at the same All-Star levels. Admittedly, the cast on his right arm was a bit of an obstacle for his opponents, but the accuracy of the new left-hand touch could not be disputed or stopped. This outstanding 6'8" forward with a thirty-foot shooting range helped to carry the league in its formative years.

BILL SHARMAN (TS)

Bill Sharman was the #2 guard in the Cousy-Sharman duo, and he was truly an amazingly accurate shooter with a deadly medium-range jump shot. This feisty 6'2" guard was ready to take anyone on who tried to push him around.

The Celtics rode his exceptional shooting for at least four NBA Championships. His career 90 percent foul shooting added icing on the cake for this hard-nosed player.

JOHN STOCKTON

I got to know John Stockton when he was still a student athlete at Gonzaga University. I had just graduated a couple of years earlier from WSU and he was finishing up his senior year at Gonzaga when I met him as his team traveled to Seattle, Washington for a game.

He was already a focused and talented young man even then who always paid attention to the fundamentals of the game and was a consummate team player. Stockton teamed with Karl "the Mailman" Malone his entire career with the Utah Jazz and led them to appearances in the playoffs every single year (which included two appearances in the NBA finals).

Stockton was a small guard by NBA standards, but he competed with the best of them. I remember one of his favorite plays was when he would pass the ball off to the wing, rub his man off the high post as he headed down to the baseline right below the basket, then circle back around to set a back pick on me. Actually, I don't know whether that was his favorite play because I remember his telling me when I joined the Utah Jazz the latter part of my career and became his teammate, "I'm so glad I don't have to set those back picks on you anymore, because I was always ducking your elbows as you tried to swing around to get me." Stockton was never shy about doing whatever it took to help his team win, even laying his body on the line as he tried to set a back pick on me.

I'd say the most enjoyable part of my career was when I became a teammate of John Stockton. He was my kind of guy, professional, focused, paying attention to details, helping his teammates to be better, and laying it all out there trying to win.

ISAIAH THOMAS

For being a small guard, Isaiah Thomas was one of the most competitive and feisty players I've ever seen. He had an incredible will to win and wasn't afraid to dust it up with anyone who stood in his way.

Isaiah came from a winning background all the way from high school, then to Indiana University with coach Bobby Knight, and then with the Detroit Pistons where he teamed with some of the most combative players I have ever had to play against—namely McFilthy and McNasty, aka Rick Mahorn and Bill Laimbeer. I'm not sure which one was which, and it doesn't matter because they were both brutal to play against.

Isaiah was one of the premiere point guards of his era in terms of the total package. He could score, play defense, assist, and run the show. After years of toiling in the shadows of the Chicago Bulls, Los Angeles Lakers, and Boston Celtics, the Detroit Pistons finally broke through with a pair of back-to-back NBA championships. Isaiah was a big reason for that. His never-say-die attitude and his willingness to play hard while leading his team to victory was a huge factor.

Of course, because I was a big guy, I didn't have to match up one-on-one with Isaiah (lucky for me because I'm sure he would have broken my ankles with his quick dribble moves), and he could tie a team up in knots as he would break down the perimeter defense and then dish off for easy layups, dunks, or short jumpers to any of a number of talented teammates. Playing against guys like that always presents a tremendous challenge. Isaiah was one of those guys!

NATE THURMOND (TS)

A constant debate used to go on about who was the best all-around center in the '60s—was it Nate Thurmond, Wilt Chamberlain, or Bill Russell? Nate Thurmond's name was always in the mix.

This versatile center's shot blocking and board work helped to take the San Francisco Warriors to their many playoff appearances. Everyone knew that it was not a good idea to get the "rise to the occasion" center angry because he would then be a supremely dominant player.

WES UNSELD

Wes Unseld was the most undersized (at least in terms of height—he was only 6'7") centers of his day. He played much bigger than he actually was because he had tremendous bulk he didn't hesitate to throw around while patrolling the paint.

A rebounder extraordinaire and outlet passer, Unseld was responsible for triggering the fast-break with the lightning quick guards with whom he played. There have been a lot of "workhorses" in the league over the years in terms of guys who played unheralded and unselfishly in the trenches, but Unseld was probably underappreciated even more than most.

He was a key catalyst in the Washington Bullets' winning the NBA championship in 1978 and returning to the championship round the next year. He teamed with Elvin "Big E" Hayes to form a dynamic duo in a very potent frontline. I tell the story elsewhere in this book of when Wes and Elvin double-teamed me as I was going for a rebound and flattened me out about six feet up in the air, before I came crashing to the hardwood in a tremendous thud. Neither one of them extended a hand to help me up, but that was life in the NBA. Wes wasn't a "leaper" by any means, so I'm going to assume that when he and Elvin double-teamed me, Elvin took me high while Wes took me low by undercutting me.

All in all, Wes Unseld was a class act, not only during his playing days, but also in management with the Washington Bullets/Wizards for years after his playing days were over. The NBA needs more guys like Wes Unseld!

BILL WALTON

Bill "The Big Redhead" Walton was a "one-of-a-kind" player during the height of his NBA career back when the Portland Trailblazers won the NBA championship in the mid-1970s. He possessed a complete package that coaches love to see in their centers—the ability to score, rebound, block shots, trigger the outlet pass, play defense, and lead his team to victory.

Walton was probably one of the very first players to cut across the "NBA culture," so to speak, when he joined the league. He sported a long mane of red hair and a beard several inches long to match. He was one of those "free living and free loving" kinds of guys who seem to be fresh out of the "flower children" generation of the 1960s. But hey, this is the NBA, and as long as you can play, perform and win, there seems to be a place for you.

I became a teammate of Bill Walton when we were both with the San Diego Clippers in 1984. We played three years together (one year in San Diego before the team moved to Los Angeles the following year), and I learned a lot about playing the center position as his teammate. He was versatile enough so he could play power forward in tandem with me playing the center position. He was a fun-loving guy, and a hoot to have as a teammate.

I remember the time when our coach, Jim Lyman, called a time out during the game, and as we were all huddling around each other, trying to listen in, Walton screamed at the top of his lungs, "Coach, I have a three in me" (meaning he wanted to take a three-point shot). Coach Lyman just smiled and asked Bill to "save it for another time." Bill Walton always kept the team loose and ready to compete.

Bill was injury-prone much of his career, so he commonly took practices off, and he didn't play every single game so he could rest his aching body. He would often coach me from the sidelines and give me a lot of tidbits on how to be a better player. While we were teammates with the Los Angeles Clippers, I would give him a ride to practice. I would meet him at a designated intersection on Pacific Coast Highway where he would tie up his bicycle to the light pole, and we'd drive to practice together. He was always positive and upbeat, and he would often try to get me to join him on the sidelines (probably so he could have company, not necessarily encouraging me to skip practice), but I didn't have that superstar status like he did, so I thought I'd best get my butt out there and practice.

It's been wonderful to see Bill Walton continue to grow and mature as a person as he's moved on to a successful TV commentator career after overcoming a severe stuttering problem he had when he was younger. That's an inspiration for a lot of people to keep on working on "their game" because you can overcome whatever challenge is facing you. Bill also went on to become an NBA champion again with the Boston Celtics in the mid-1980s. Many people wonder how great a career Walton would have had if he had stayed healthy throughout, but it's safe to say that he nevertheless ranks right up there with the all-time greats by being a two-time NBA champion and Hall of Famer.

JERRY WEST (TS)

Jerry West is the third part to the argument, "Which player is the best of the big guards?" Many mature fans feel that "Mr. Clutch," as he was called for his many game-winning shots, was the best of the Oscar "Big O" Robertson/Michael Jordan argument as to who was the all time best.

Whatever the choice, Jerry West was a super scorer and leader of the Los Angeles Lakers during the '60s and early '70s. His quickness of hands on defense and the speed with which he could get his extremely accurate shots off marked West as one of the game's greatest.

LENNY WILKENS

I didn't have the pleasure of watching Lenny Wilkens, the player, but I did have the pleasure of being coached by Lenny Wilkens, the coach, when I was with the Seattle SuperSonics in the early '80s. Anybody who knows basketball history can tell you that Lenny Wilkens was one of the all-time great players in NBA history and then he went on to become the all-time winningest coach in NBA history. That's quite an accomplishment!

Wilkens was one of my favorite coaches because he really understood the mental makeup of the NBA player. I played with the Sonics just a year after they won their one and only NBA championship in 1979. When I was with them, the team was still stocked with NBA championship caliber players in every position, and Lenny Wilkens did a masterful job of continuing to coach the team in spite of missing a couple of the key players from the championship team. I love the fact that he treated us like men instead of little boys, but at the same time, he had big expectations for you to conduct yourself like a man and be a professional. It was a great way for me to break into the league—to be coached by Lenny Wilkens.

Wilkens went on to have a very lengthy coaching career, and he was successful at virtually every stop along the way. His teams always seemed to be competitive and in the hunt for another title, which miraculously somehow eluded him the rest of his coaching career. It just goes to show you how difficult it is to win an NBA championship. You have to have all the right pieces in place, and then you need a great coach like Lenny Wilkens.

JAMES WORTHY

In the breakneck speed of the daunting fast-break of the "Showtime Lakers," James Worthy was probably the fastest and most valuable member. He possessed catlike quickness and sprinter speed to get from one end of the court to the other for one of his patented Tomahawk dunks. Playing with Magic Johnson didn't hurt, but Worthy showed he was able to carry the team from time to time by putting up tremendous numbers himself.

Worthy was one of those rare blends of athletic ability, intelligence, teamwork, unselfishness, a hard work ethic, and a player who was coachable. As an NCAA champion at the University of North Carolina before joining the NBA, Worthy was a winner everywhere he went.

Worthy managed to get his share of the limelight even on a star-studded team like the Los Angeles Lakers of the 1980s. That's saying something in itself, but he was consistently productive, game after game and year after year. The Lakers won multiple championships during James Worthy's tenure with the Los Angeles Lakers.

I don't think there was ever an adequate defense devised that could slow down James Worthy. It seemed like he was everywhere at once; he was so quick that he gave his defenders fits. He was also a pretty good defender in his own right in playing the passing lanes and coming up with steals and putting pressure on his man.

After an illustrious career, Worthy moved on to become a bona fide TV commentator for NBA basketball games.

SUMMARY

There you have it—the complete list of the NBA's All-Time Fifty Greatest Players along with "Satch" Sanders, Lenny Wilkens, and my perspectives on what it was like to play against and be on the court with them at the same time. Like anything in life, I am sure we all had our strategies in place to go out there and play hard and well against these great players… or to risk being embarrassed.

I want to say a special thanks to Tom "Satch" Sanders and to one of my favorite NBA coaches and Hall of Famer Lenny Wilkens for their contributions to this section. Their insight and "real life" experience of being with and playing against the best has really added something special to this section of the book for me and I hope it has for you as well.

ABOUT THE AUTHOR

James Donaldson is a Washington State University graduate ('79). After an outstanding basketball career with WSU, he went on to play professional basketball in the NBA with the Seattle Supersonics, San Diego/L.A. Clippers, Dallas Mavericks, New York Knicks, and Utah Jazz. He also played for several teams in the European Leagues in Spain, Italy, and Greece, and he toured with The Harlem Globetrotters to wrap up his career. James was an NBA All-Star in 1988 while playing center for the Dallas Mavericks. In 2006, James was inducted into the Pac-10 Sports Hall of Fame and also the Washington State University Athletic Hall of Fame. In 2010, James was elected as a board member for the NBA Retired Players Association.

James established The Donaldson Clinic in January 1990 (shortly after a career-threatening knee injury) with the idea that he would eventually become a physical therapist. He is a strong advocate for Women & Minority owned businesses and is very involved with various Chambers of Commerce. He understands what it takes to sustain a strong business environment that is conducive to the success of businesses overall. He also serves as a coach for other small business owners.

Today, James devotes the majority of his time to various community activities and to the operations of The Donaldson Clinic. James frequently conducts speaking engagements (motivational, inspirational, educational) for organizations, schools, and youth groups.

In 2009, James was a candidate for the office of Mayor for the City of Seattle. He had a strong fourth place finish in a crowded field of eight candidates. It was the first time James ran for an elected office in the world of politics, and he continues to work closely with several elected officials in regards to politics, youth, and educational issues in Seattle.

In 2010, James was the recipient of the NBA Legends of Basketball ABC Award, awarded for outstanding contributions in *Athletics–Business–Community.*

James is a long-time resident of the Magnolia neighborhood in Seattle. He believes in being a role model for success and professionalism to the scores of young people to whom he devotes so much of his time. He currently serves on several boards and committees and is a member of many organizations.

James believes in developing relationships that create a "Win-Win" environment for everyone involved, and in being the best he can be!

For more information about James Donaldson or to request he speak at your event, contact him at:

WWW.STANDINGABOVETHECROWD.COM
JAMESD@STANDINGABOVETHECROWD.COM
1-800-745-3161 (VOICEMAIL & FAX)